Jacob of Sarug's Homilies on the Six Days of Creation: The Fourth Day

Texts from Christian Late Antiquity

52

TeCLA (Texts from Christian Late Antiquity) is a series presenting ancient Christian texts both in their original languages and with accompanying contemporary English translations.

Jacob of Sarug's Homilies on the Six Days of Creation: The Fourth Day

Edited and Translated by

Edward G Mathews Jr

2018

Gorgias Press LLC, 954 River Road, Piscataway, NJ, 08854, USA

www.gorgiaspress.com

Copyright © 2018 by Gorgias Press LLC

All rights reserved under International and Pan-American Copyright Conventions. No part of this publication may be reproduced, stored in a retrieval system or transmitted in any form or by any means, electronic, mechanical, photocopying, recording, scanning or otherwise without the prior written permission of Gorgias Press LLC.

2018

ISBN 978-1-4632-3912-1   **ISSN 1935-6846**

```
Library of Congress Cataloging-in-Publication
Data

A Cataloging-in-Publication Record is available
from the Library of Congress.
```

Printed in the United States of America

TABLE OF CONTENTS

Table of Contents v
Abbreviations vii
Introduction 1
   Outline 1
   Summary 5
Text and Translation 7
Homily 71d: On the Fashioning of Creation: The Fourth Day 8
   I.   God creates the Luminaries and fills them with Light from the First Day 8
   II.   God lays out the courses for each of the luminaries 12
   III. The Erroneous Teaching of the Chaldeans 16
   IV. The Role of the Sun and the Moon in Plant Germination 22
   V.   The Moon is a Type of a Human Being 26
   VI. The Sun is a type of God 28
   VII. The Heavens Proclaim the Glory of the Creator 32
   VIII. On the Fourth Day God Created the Moon Full 36
   IX. God set the Luminaries in Continuous Motion along Specific Courses 40
   X.   God gave to each of the Luminaries its own Particular Glory 44
   XI. God established the Times and Seasons by the Sun and the Moon 46
Bibliography of Works Cited 51
   Primary Texts 51
   Secondary Works 52
Index 55
   Names and Themes 55
   Biblical References 58

ABBREVIATIONS

Bedjan	P. Bedjan, *Homiliae Selectae Mar-Jacobi Sarugensis* (see BIBLIOGRAPHY)
BETL	Bibliotheca Ephemeridum Theologicarum Lovaniensium
CBOTS	Coniectanea Biblica. Old Testament Series
CSCO	Corpus Scriptorum Christianorum Orientalium
FOTC	Fathers of the Church
OCA	*Orientalia Christiana Analecta*
OCP	*Orientalia Christiana Periodica*
OS	*L'Orient Syrien*
OtSt	*Oudtestamentische Studien*
PdO	*Parole de l'Orient*
PO	Patrologia Orientalis
S	*Sobornost*
SC	Sources Chrétiennes
TFCLA	Texts from Christian Late Antiquity

INTRODUCTION

> INFORMATION ON THIS HOMILY
> Homily Title: Homily on the Fashioning of Creation, The Fourth Day
> Source of Text: *Homiliae Selectae Mar-Jacobi Sarugensis*, edited by Paul Bedjan (Paris-Leipzig: Harrassowitz, 1907, 2nd ed. Piscataway: Gorgias Press, 2006), vol. 3, pp. 60–79. [Homily 71d]
> Lines: 386 [1181–1566]

OUTLINE

The text translated here in this fascicule constitutes the fourth installment of the long *Mêmrâ on the Fashioning of Creation*, composed in the late fifth-early sixth century by the bishop and prolific poet and theologian Mār Jacob of Sarug (c.451–521). This long *mêmrâ* comments on the six days of creation as found recorded in the first chapter of the canonical book of Genesis.[1] However, as we have already noted in a previous fascicle, this *Mêmrâ* is technically a *Heptaemeron* as Jacob also discusses the seventh day, the day of the Sabbath rest.[2]

The section translated here in this fascicule, which comprises lines 1181–1566 of the original *mêmrâ*, provides the reader with

---

[1] The entire text was first published in P. Bedjan, *Homiliae Selectae Mar-Jacobi Sarugensis*, III.1–151. The first three days were reprinted in separate fascicules, with English translations, in Mathews, *Jacob of Sarug's Homilies on the Six Days of Creation: The First Day*, idem., *Jacob of Sarug's Homilies on the Six Days of Creation: The Second Day*, and idem., *Jacob of Sarug's Homilies on the Six Days of Creation: The Third Day*.

[2] Mathews, *Jacob of Sarug's Homilies on the Six Days of Creation: The Second Day*, 2, n. 4, with reference to Bedjan's text.

Jacob's poetic meditation on the fourth day of creation as recorded in Genesis 1:14–19. On this day God created the two great luminaries, the sun "to rule over the day," and the moon, along with the stars of the heavens, "to rule over the night".[3]

As has been the case in the preceding fascicules of this *mêmrâ*, it seems that Jacob may have been aware, or at least availed himself, of only a single written source other than the Bible, and that is the *Commentary on Genesis*, composed by his predecessor and theological mentor, Ephrem the Syrian (c.306–373).[4] While Jansma, in the article just cited, catalogues a number of previous and contemporary writers on these initial chapters of Genesis, he is rather situating Jacob in his context than positing any of them as direct sources.[5] Whether Jacob was in fact aware or not of any of these, there is no concrete evidence of it in any of the parts of this *mêmrâ* that have been translated to this point.

As was the case with his coverage of the first three days, Jacob follows the biblical text very closely and, while his meditation introduces to the hearer/reader much that is not directly related in the short text of Genesis, he differs very little from what Ephrem said in his *Commentary on Genesis*, although he always expands upon, and often shows further development than his main inspiration. Above all, Jacob continues to exhort his hearers/readers that the primary teaching of this Genesis account is that it is God – and God alone – who made everything, and it is He who continues to guide and to oversee all things according to the patterns He set down in these first six days. This is the primary error of the Chaldeans, whose teaching is widely followed by so many peoples, who

---

[3] See summary in T. Jansma, "L'Hexaméron de Jacques de Sarug," 23–27.

[4] R. Tonneau, ed. *Sancti Ephraem Syri in Genesim et in Exodum commentarii*. English translation by E. G. Mathews, Jr., in *St. Ephrem the Syrian: Selected Prose Works*, 67–213.

[5] T. Jansma, "L'Hexaméron de Jacques de Sarug," 129–162; he also treats some of Jacob's contemporary Syrian writers, including Narsai, on pp. 253–278. His footnotes are very useful, however, for parallels to other writers, some later than Jacob, who are not included in the notes to our translation, below.

thought that the sun moved itself and caused the movement of the other spheres, and thus denied any creator or source.[6]

Following a fairly wide-spread tradition, Jacob, as does his mentor Ephrem, states that when God set about to create the sun, the moon and the stars, He created the appropriate size spheres and then placed within them that very same light that had been created on the first day. This light is now dimmed to varying degrees in each of its new receptacles: the sun clearly the brightest, then the moon, and then the various stars that each had their own level of illumination.[7] In this portion of the homily, Jacob gives the impression that the entire light created on the first day is now apportioned into its new receptacles, but one must remember from the portion of this *mêmrâ* dealing with the second day that that original light still existed above the firmament where it was seen separately by Paul, Ezekiel and Stephen.[8]

God then set these luminaries on their individual courses, and these courses then determined the various times that occur on the earth: not only day and night, the times of work and of rest for humans, feeding and grazing for animals, but for each of the four seasons. In addition to the seasons of sowing and harvest, the sun and moon, in particular, are both important for the growth of all vegetation: after the earth puts forth the first steps of germination, it is the moon that provides the first impetus of growth, and then the sun takes over and causes the vegetation to grow and reach full maturity. The sole exception to this is everything that was created on the third day, when God commanded the earth to put forth vegetation – n.b., before the existence of the sun and the moon! And Jacob reiterates here in this portion of his homily what he had previously said on the third day – again following that which he had received from Ephrem –, that everything that was created on that third day was created instantaneously in its full-grown form.[9]

---

[6] See, below, ll. 1249–1276.

[7] See, below, ll. 1511–1536.

[8] Mathews, *Jacob of Sarug's Homilies on the Six Days of Creation: The Second Day*, 683–694, 735–764.

[9] See, below, ll. 1450–1452, and note ad loc.

In addition to the account of the creation of the luminaries, Jacob teaches his hearers/readers that the sun and the moon also serve as types of God and man, respectively. The sun rises with its full light and heat and maintains both as it traverses through the sky throughout the entire day, depicting the God who does not change, who is "the same yesterday, today and forever".[10] The moon, on the other hand, waxes and wanes, depicting the ages of humankind, who is born, grows up to maturity, and from then gradually grows old and feeble. This should stand as a warning to young people to be humble when they are young and strong, because it is only a matter of time before old age sets in.[11]

Once the creation of the heavenly hosts has been completed and all the various luminaries are moving along their designated courses directing the various seasons and times, Jacob invokes the first verse of Psalm 19, calling on his hearers/readers to join all of creation in marveling at what God has wrought: "The heavens proclaim the glory of God, and the firmament makes known the work of His hands"![12] As the heavens and the firmament do, so too should humankind, for whom God created all that He created. Again, following his mentor St. Ephrem, Jacob highlights the primary purpose of all creation, and of mankind, in particular – to give praise to the Creator and Lord of all. To the creation of mankind on the sixth day we approach closer and closer, but next we move to the birds and the animals on the fifth day.

As was the case with our translation to days two and three, this translation of day four is the first into any modern language. A summary does exist in the article of Jansma cited above,[13] but there has been no full translation. I hope that, thanks to the careful and diligent efforts of the editors, most notably Sebastian Brock and Melonie Schmierer-Lee, my errors and omissions have been reduced to a minimum.

---

[10] Hebrews 13:8.
[11] See, below, ll. 1338–1360.
[12] See, below, ll. 1403–1436.
[13] T. Jansma, "L'Hexaméron de Jacques de Sarug," 23–27.

Summary

I. God creates the Luminaries and fills them with Light from the First Day (1181–1214)

II. God lays out the courses for each of the luminaries (1215–1248)

III. The Erroneous Teaching of the Chaldeans (1249–1298)

IV. The Role of the Sun and the Moon in Plant Germination (1299–1332)

V. The Moon is a Type of a Human Being (1333–1360)

VI. The Sun is a type of God (1361–1402)

VII. The Heavens Proclaim the Glory of the Creator (1403–1436)

VIII. On the Fourth Day God Created the Moon Full (1437–1466)

IX. God set the Luminaries in Continuous Motion along Specific Courses (1467–1508)

X. God gave to each of the Luminaries its own Particular Glory (1509–1540)

XI. God established the Times and Seasons by the Sun and the Moon (1541–1566)

TEXT AND TRANSLATION

Homily 71d: On the Fashioning of Creation: The Fourth Day

I. God creates the Luminaries and fills them with Light from the First Day

1181 Then,[1] on the fourth day, the Lord created the luminaries,
And He placed the light[2] into these moving spheres.
God said, "Let there be", and all the luminaries came to be: Gen 1:14
the sun, the moon, and the stars, all arrayed in their various forms.
1185 The sun became as it were the king of all the luminaries;
the moon came to be and [God] bound it to its course along with
    its yoke-mate.
The stars came to be "for signs and for seasons,
and for days and for years," as well as for [other] time intervals.   Gen 1:14
[God] made the sun to be "ruler over the day",[3]   Gen 1:16

---

[1] Syr., *hāydēn*. This might sound like an odd way to begin a homily, but the reader must remember that this is not the beginning but is actually the middle of a long, single homily on the six days of creation.

[2] That is, the light that was created on the first day. Jacob discusses this light earlier in this homily (see lines 465–520, 699–764, 1167–1180), as well as below (lines 1193–1196, 1201–1202, 1209–1214). Here, as in so many other places, he seems to follow above all the teaching of his intellectual mentor, St. Ephrem; cf. Ephrem, *Commentary on Genesis*, I.9. This teaching seems to have been preserved in the School of Edessa as it is also found in the homilies of Narsai; cf. his *Homilies on Creation*, I.61–66, III.177–178, who may have inherited it either from Ephrem or from Basil; see his *Homilies on the Hexaemeron*, VI.2. It was also taught by Eghishē, *Commentary on Genesis*, 26–27, as well as by Theodoret, see his *Questions on the Octateuch*, xiv, who adds in *Question* xvi that it was necessary to put this light in muted form into the spheres for the animals who "have eyes and could not have tolerated the excessively bright light. But when this [first light] was apportioned among the lesser and the greater lights, it emitted a brightness commensurate with the vision of the animals." Jacob himself seems to maintain this same position in *Jacob of Sarug's Homily on The Second Day*, 741–745.

B 71

ܘܥܠ ܐܘܡܢܐ ܕܒܪܝܬܐ: ܩܘܡܐ .ܘ.

60

ܘܒܝܘܡ ܗܕܢ ܗܘܐ ܢܗܪܐ ܕܙܒܢܐ:
ܘܩܡܘ ܠܢܘܗܪܐ ܕܥܠܡ ܚܝܠܐ ܘܟܘܟܒܐ܀
ܐܡܪ ܐܠܗܐ ܘܢܗܘܘܢ ܘܗܘܘ ܦܠܐ ܢܗܡܢ:
ܫܡܫܐ ܘܣܗܪܐ ܘܟܘܟܒܐ ܥܡ ܬܪܝܢ ܚܐܣܟܡܬܘܢ܀
ܗܘܐ ܕܝܢ ܫܡܫܐ ܩܐܡܟ ܡܠܟܐ ܘܦܠܐ ܢܗܡܢ:
ܘܗܘܐ ܣܗܪܐ ܘܩܢܐ ܚܙܘܗ ܥܡ ܟܠ ܐܘܝܢ܀
ܘܗܘܐ ܩܘܡܐ ܘܠܠܐܘܬܐ ܕܐܪܥܐ ܠܗܘܘܢ:
ܘܠܣܒܥܕܐ ܐܦ ܠܥܢܬܐ ܘܠܚܒܪܢܐ܀

1181

1185

61

ܠܓܒܪܗ ܠܫܡܫܐ ܘܢܘܗܐ ܥܘܠ ܥܠܐ ܥܡܐ:

---

[3] Not the exact wording of the Peshitta, either here at Genesis 1:16, or at Psalm 136:8.

1190   to govern it, move about in it and take its delight in it.
And He made the moon to preside as "ruler over the night",[4]   Gen 1:16
and along with it the stars that proceed along their paths.[5]
He commanded that light which had spread throughout creation,
and it entered and took its place entirely[6] within those beautiful spheres.
1195   [The light] was collected, gathered together, and then confined therein,
it became an orb and He yoked it to the course of the great dome.[7]
The two great luminaries and the stars He set upon the firmament,[8]

---

[4] Closer than the previous, but still not exactly the wording of the Peshitta at Genesis or at Psalm 136:9; both are likely due to metrical reasons.

[5] Cf. Genesis 1:16, and Psalm 136:9.

[6] This adverb must refer to the light filling up the spheres 'entirely' rather than to all the light fitting into these spheres; cf. introduction, above, p. 3.

[7] I.e., the firmament, though Jacob does not use this word for the firmament when he discusses its creation and its form in *Jacob of Sarug's Homily on The Second Day*. Balai, *Sermons on Joseph* 11.6, already spoke of the "comely dome of the firmament"; cited from M. Sokoloff, *A Syriac Lexicon*, 654b.

[8] Here Jacob follows the biblical text and – presumably – Ephrem (see his *Commentary on Genesis*, I.23, 26, but he does not really take a clear position), that the luminaries were placed upon the firmament. Narsai, however, explicitly denies this, maintaining that while the stars were hung upon the firmament, the sun and moon were suspended from it like lamps; see his *Homilies on Creation*, III.179–180, as well as I.63–64. Diodore of Tarsus argues on the analogy of Adam who was not affixed to the earth, but placed to dwell on the earth, so too the luminaries were not affixed to the firmament, but set to move around within the firmament; see F. Petit, *Catenae Graece II*, 51. After a long discussion about three possible options, Eusebius of Emesa decides that the luminaries were not attached to the very firmament but were placed very near to it; see Eusebius of Emesa, *Commentary on Genesis*, 38–43, and discussion in M. Alexandre, *Le Commencement du livre Genèse I–V*, 141–142, where she also notes Jewish parallels. The Armenian vardapet Eghishē, *Commentary on Genesis*,

---

28–29, does not say explicitly where they were placed, but does state that they "were not established immovably (Arm., *ansharzhapēs*).

and He made them as rulers over the days and the nights,
that the sun may serve the day like a judge,
1200 and the moon and the stars may be like ministers for the night.
From that light that had existed for the [first] three days,
these luminaries came to be for the service of the world.
They were for the firmament like beautiful adornments,
while for the path of the world they were like moving candles,
1205 as rulers for both days and nights,
and for the change of all the seasons they became ministers.
For inhabited regions full of darkness they became lanterns,
and for the ministry of this great house,[9] towering lamps.
That light hastened, entered in and took its place within the luminaries[10]
1210 that in them it may reign over creatures and their temporal changes.
The sun, the moon and the stars that came to be [were now] completely light,
that [light] about which God had earlier commanded, "Let there be light." Gen 1:3
That light came to be and its brightness served for three days,[11]
but it was then distributed among the luminaries on the fourth day.[12]

II. GOD LAYS OUT THE COURSES FOR EACH OF THE LUMINARIES

1215 The Maker set out by these moving spheres
the entire course of this world and of its temporal changes:
cold and heat, summer and winter in their seasons,
and the cycle of night and day on their pathways.
He joined the globe[13] onto an orderly course that is full of wonder,

---

[9] A phrase that Jacob has already used to designate the earth; see *Jacob of Sarug's Homily on The Second Day*, 667, 681, 712, 754; *Jacob of Sarug's Homily on The Third Day*, 1082, 1084, etc.

[10] See line 1194, above.

[11] See Jacob's earlier discussion in lines 1171–1180; see also *Jacob of Sarug's Homily on The Third Day*, 44–45.

[12] Again, see introduction, above, p. 3.

---

[13] Syr., *mawzaltā*, usually used generically of any celestial sphere, but here it clearly refers specifically to the sun; see also line 1256, below.

1220	and He set a boundary for it as to how and how far it might travel.
	"The sun came forth like a bride-groom from his bridal chamber,
	and began to leap like a strong man running along its path"; Psalm 19:5
	it came forth from the end of the world as soon as it came to be,
	from the head of that region that brings forth the light.[14]
1225	Within that boundary there He made [the light]; He made it
	beyond the world, but He sent it to go provide for the world.
	In that place from which it dawned from that time forward,
	He forged it, filled it with light and sent it to the earth.
	He made it a lamp so that that once dark house might be served by it,
1230	to drive away the darkness when it enters therein.
	It went out from the east but took hold of the south by the course of its path,
	the west then took it in, spread out its wings and enveloped it.
	Its hiding place is in the north; it fixed its path along its regions:
	in the east, the south, the west and the north wherein it hurried along.
1235	On the fourth day these four regions were named,
	for prior to this day these regions had not been known.
	Before the sun dawned from it there was no east,
	nor was there a west until [the sun] set and was concealed in it.
	On the fourth day the luminaries hurried along their paths,
1240	then the regions received their designated names.
	The luminaries lined up like advancing legions,
	to lead the hosts along the path of the heavens.
	For all the stars, He counted their number and set down their names,[15]
	so that each of them might proceed just as it was commanded:

---

[14] Cf. Psalm 19:6.
[15] Psalm 147:4.

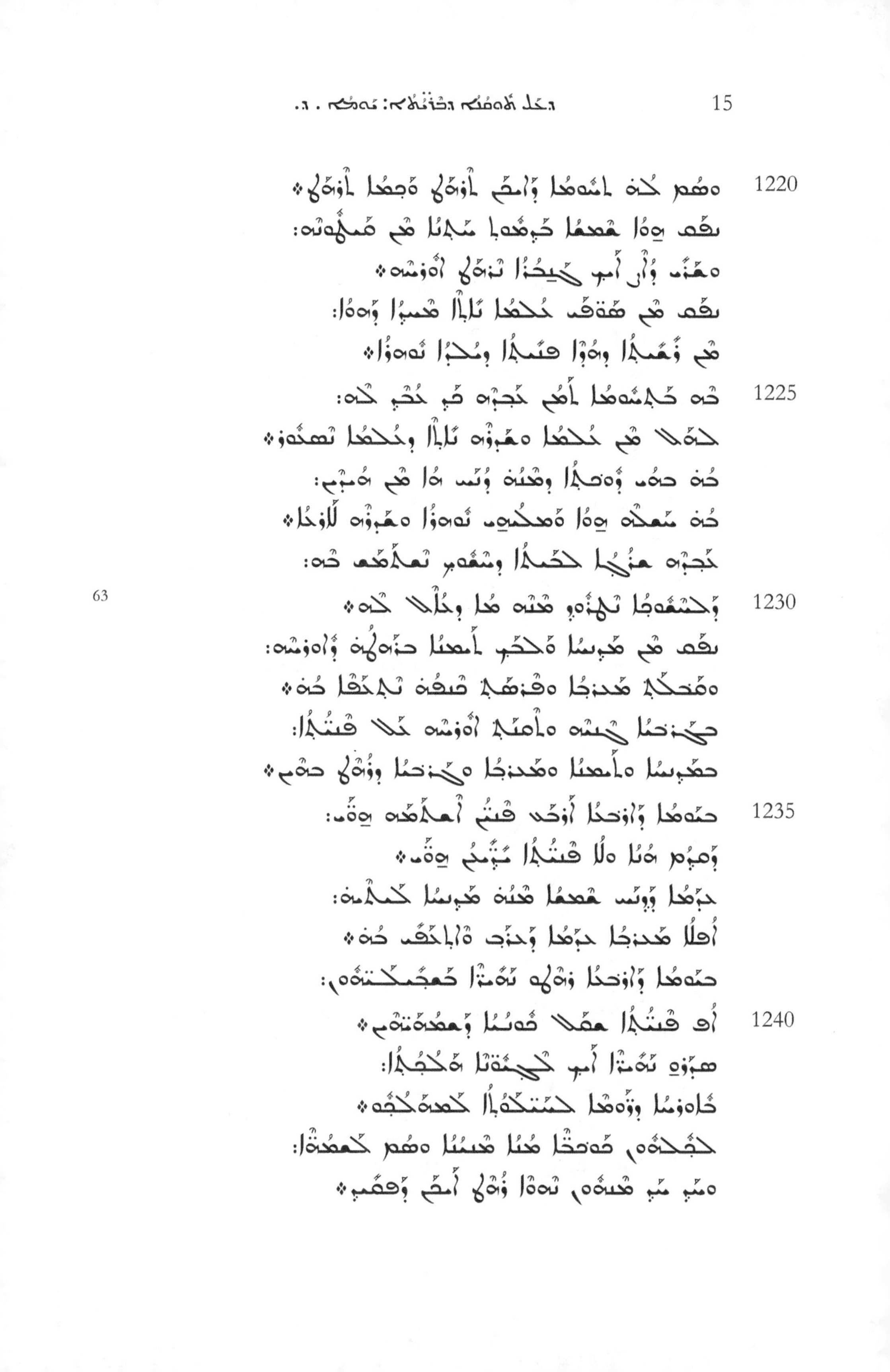

16 THE SIX DAYS OF CREATION: THE FOURTH DAY

1245 for the course of the seasons and for all the other temporal changes,
and for the ways of summer and winter in their various forms.
Governance such as this is above all knowledge,
above all wisdom and above all senses of earthly beings.

III. THE ERRONEOUS TEACHING OF THE CHALDEANS

The Chaldeans went astray by this orb that with its finite course;[16]
1250 they thought they understood, but they did not understand as they thought.
They went astray by this because they saw beautiful things arrayed along with it,
and because they saw that the movements controlled by it were many,
and because of the throng of hosts bound to it,
and the activity that is naturally instigated by it.
1255 They saw that in wisdom it was higher than any other existing thing,
but those foolish men thought that this globe[17] had created itself.

---

[16] A difficult phrase; Syr., *malyat raḥṭâ*, literally, "full of motion" or "filled/completed in its course". I take it to mean that Jacob finds the error of the Chaldeans in assigning deity to the sun which has a defined, limited course that it is clearly made to follow by a higher being. See his argument that follows: even though the sun does in fact exert control over other smaller, lower objects it is nonetheless the power of God that controls the sun and consequently even all these other objects.

[17] Cf. line 1219, above, and note ad loc.

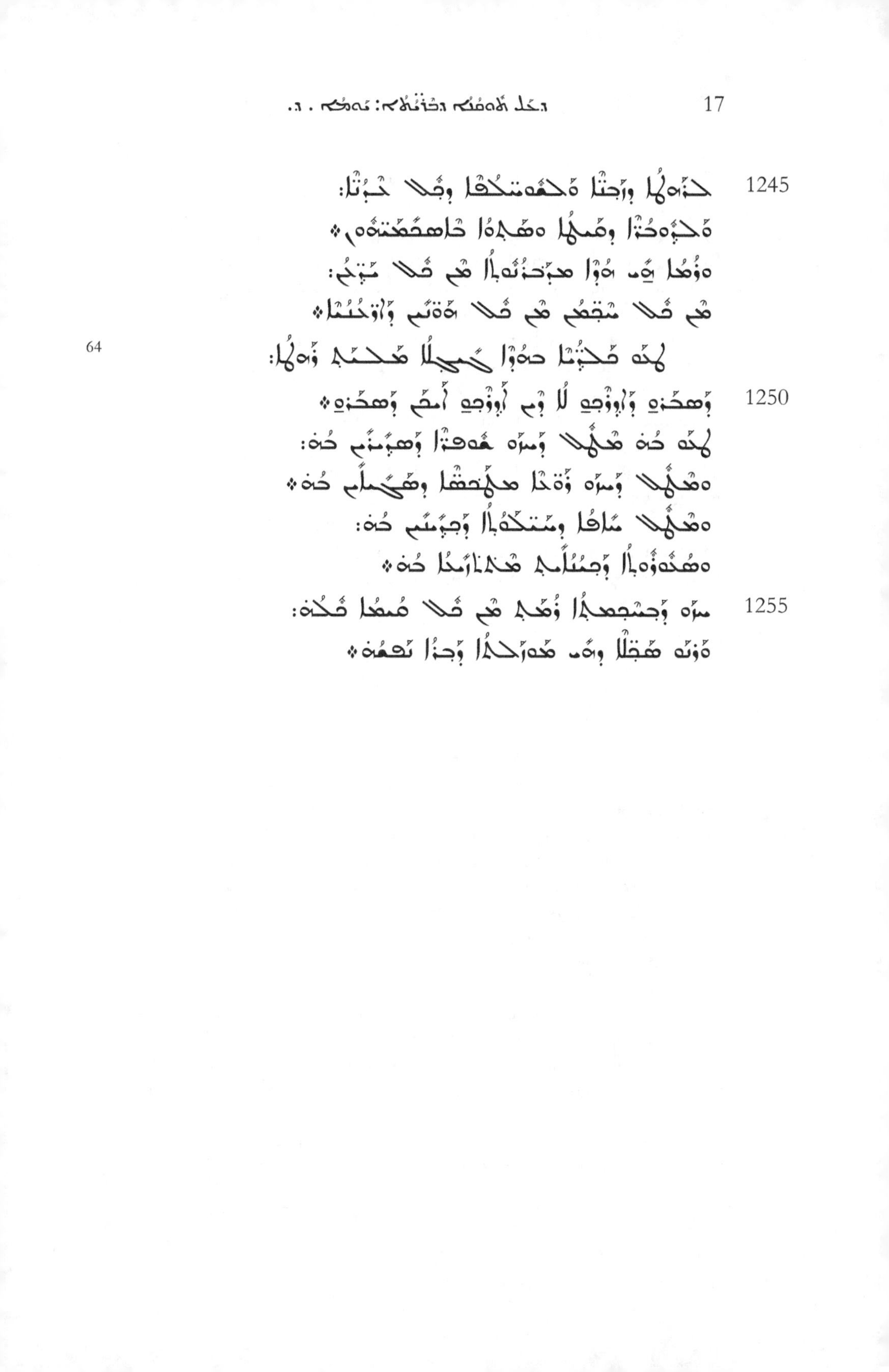

They did not comprehend that it was the hidden power[18] of the
     Godhead[19]
that had bound it and given it movement along its paths.
Rather, they considered that its governance was from itself,
1260 and that in the Zodiac it had the power to make a thing move.[20]
And these stars that the Creator had set out for times,
the [Chaldeans] assign as various things for mankind.
They marveled at what was made, how beautiful it was and were
     amazed at it,
but they remained ignorant that there is a Creator and that He is
     wise.
1265 The Chaldeans posited fates and fortunes as well as horoscopes
in their writings, as if the world existed by them.
That nature that was [in fact] an obedient servant,[21]
they considered to be a Lord and a governor.
Can a star give a crown to kings or a throne to princes?

---

[18] The hidden aspects of God, including His power, are those beyond the capacity of human understanding that have not yet been revealed, see T. Kollamparampil, *Salvation in Christ according to Jacob of Serugh*, 73–75. This particular phrase, "hidden power", is also part of an underlying anti-Arian polemic that Jacob sometimes conducts, see T. Bou Mansour, *La théologie de Jacques de Saroug*, I, 17–22, where he also notes that in many cases *haylâ*/power and *remzâ*/sign are practically interchangeable; see further, below, n. 45.

[19] Or, "Divinity".

[20] Cf. Wisdom of Solomon 13:1–9; the worship of the heavenly bodies was still a danger in biblical times, cf. Deuteronomy 4:19. The Chaldeans and their pervasive astrological teaching was also a common foil for Christian apologists. Basil, *Hexaemeron*, IV.5–7, is a more traditional diatribe against Chaldean astrology.

[21] An epithet used previously of the sea; see line 963 in Mathews, *Jacob of Sarug's Homilies on the Six Days of Creation: The Third Day*, 22–23.

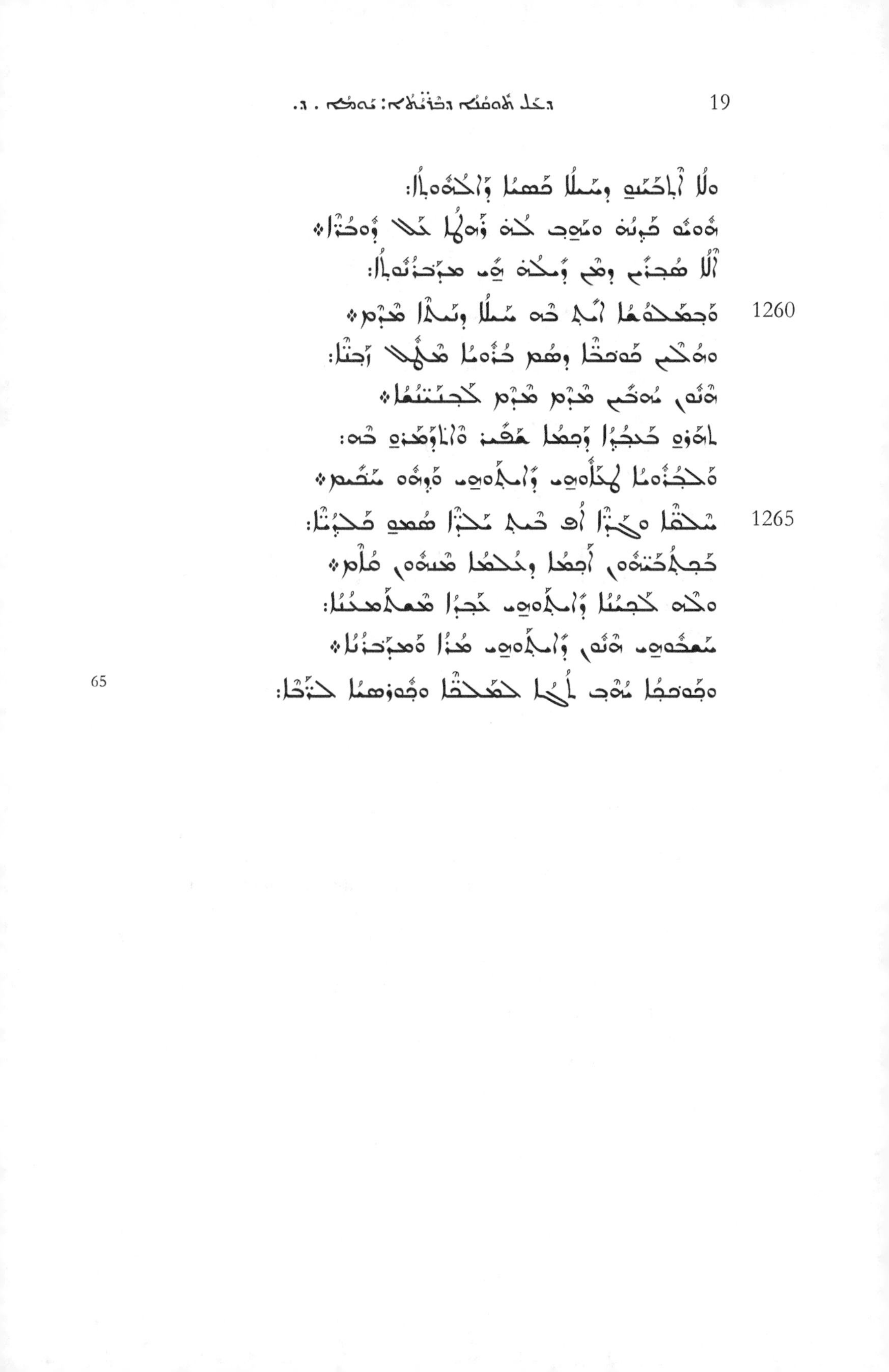

1270	high rank or authority to rulers?
	Is a star able to grant wealth or poverty,
	reputation or glory, lowliness or shame on its own?
	In knowledge the Chaldeans were not knowledgeable,
	and by their wisdom they found themselves to be unwise.
1275	For who, being so wise, would go so far astray
	as to give glory to a thing that was made but not to its artisan?
	That Maker who gave to nature all its variety,
	is the [sole] one able to grant it or not.
	If a nature possesses anything, its Lord has granted it,
1280	for it is itself unable to give anything to its companions.
	That Creator gave heat to the fire,
	but if you warm yourself by it you do not give [fire] the glory.
	Nor, even if the fire is considered to have a power,
	is it able to burn without the Lord – *its* Lord – willing it.
1285	The Chaldeans threw the young men into the furnace,[22]
	but when its Lord commanded the fire, it put forth dew.[23]
	And there is neither blame nor censure for the fire,
	for to burn or not to burn does not belong to itself.
	When the fire came down and consumed the water in the trench,[24]

---

[22] Cf. Daniel 3:21.

[23] This curious action stems from a reading that seems to be unique to the Peshitta. While the LXX at Daniel 3:49 (there is no corresponding Hebrew text here) reads "Then the angel of the Lord went down into the furnace to those with Azariah", the corresponding verse in the Peshitta, reads "For the angel *of the dew* came down with Hananiah, Azariah, and Mishael, into the midst of the fiery furnace (emphasis added)"; R. Taylor, *Peshitta of Daniel*, 115, 119, only lists the variant reading, he offers no comment. Jacob here omits mention of the angel, probably due to the verse limits as well as because the mediation of the angel is not necessary for Jacob's point here which is to demonstrate the sole rulership of God in this and in every matter. See also Jacob's *Homily on Daniel and his Companions*, Bedjan, *Homiliae Selectae Mar-Jacobi Sarugensis*, II.121, line 20: "The [three] youths were enveloped in dew in the furnace."

[24] Cf. 1 Kings 18:38.

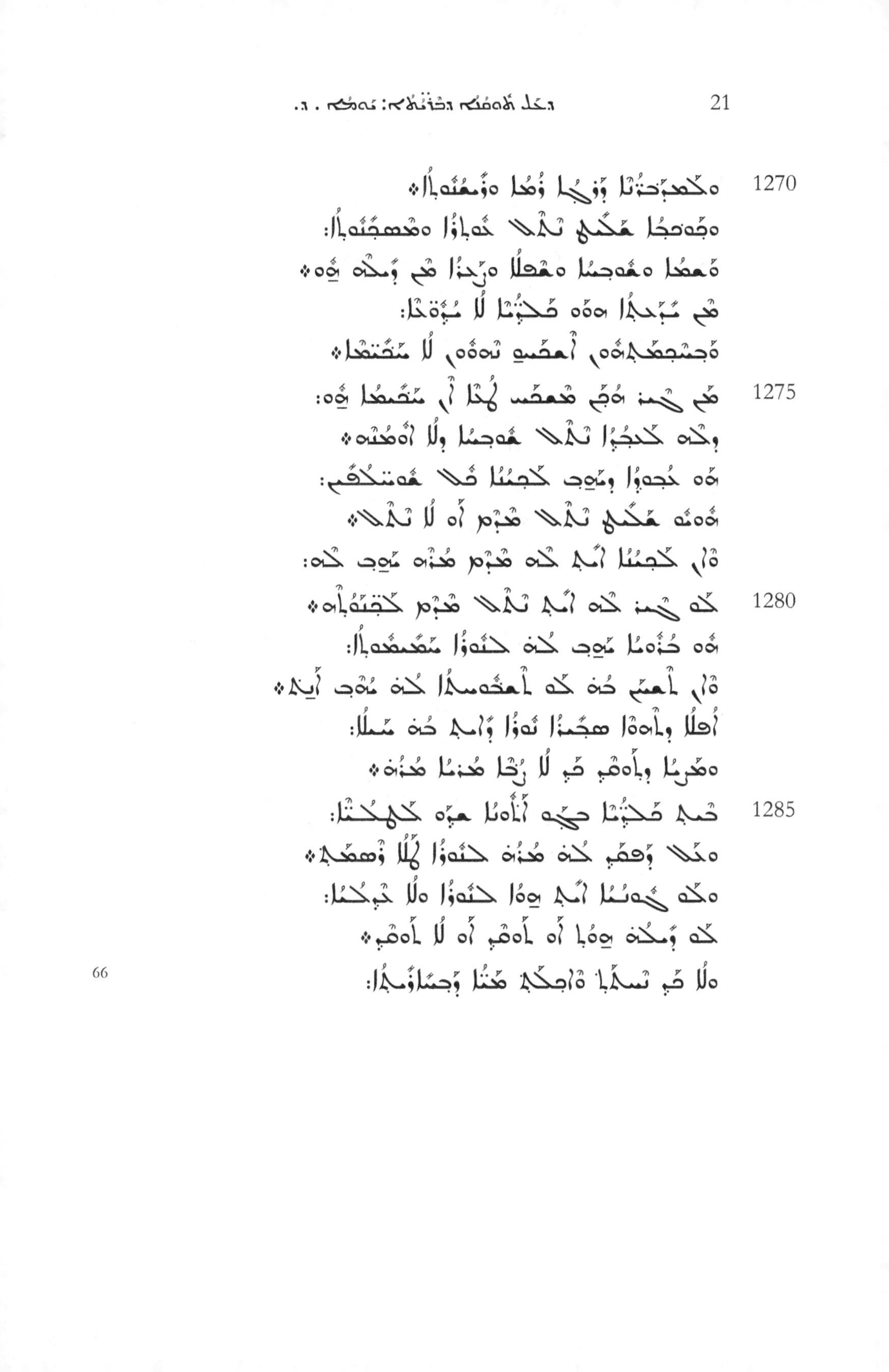

1290 it was not given praise by those who were looking on,
    nor when the young men entered into it and it grew cool among the Chaldeans,
  was it to be faulted when its flame died down.
  For it has no power either to burn or to die down,
  for fire has always had a ruler and a Lord.
1295 [Only] if He gives the command does it consume the water in the trench,
  or does it fear to burn a single hair in the midst of the furnace.
  Thus, the Lord of natures is the ruler over His creation,
  and at His command everything proceeds according to its activity.

IV. THE ROLE OF THE SUN AND THE MOON IN PLANT GERMINATION

  The Creator placed various things among His varied creation
1300 to be like handmaidens for the service of the world.
  It is as if to say the sun and the moon are two ministers:
  the moon to bring forth every sort of vegetation and the sun to ripen them.
  [God] placed in the moon cold and moisture,
  and a pleasant breeze to make all vegetation germinate and sprout.
1305 And He placed in the sun warmth and dryness
  to ripen fruits and to give taste to all vegetation.
  Thus, by the pleasant breeze all vegetation might flourish,
  and the heat of the sun might endue them with every color.
  Color, smell and taste of vegetation are in the sun,

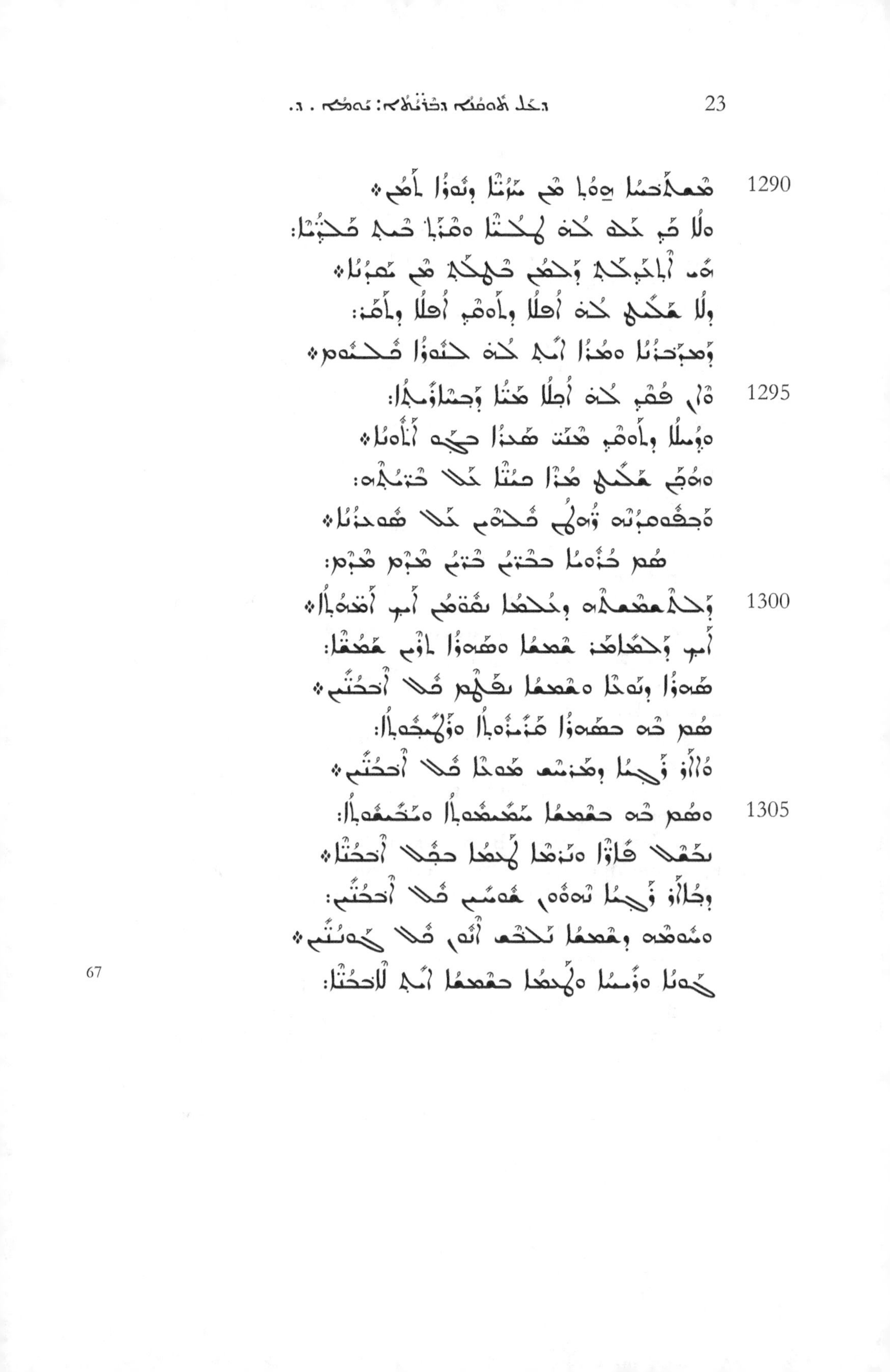

1310   while germination and growth are placed in the moon.
       The Creator has given this action to [their] nature,
       [that nature] can do nothing [of itself] as we have said[25].
       Read in the blessings with which Moses blessed the children of Jacob,
       for it is written there "from the vegetation that the moon puts forth".[26]   Deut 33:14
1315   That Maker provided the air to be its germinator,
       in this action that its Lord gave it, it proceeds continuously.
       Not because Moses said, "the vegetation that the moon puts forth",
       should you think that the moon is capable of making anything sprout,
       for when anything grew it was the earth that first pushed it forth,
1320   for the moon had not [yet] been created, nor had its companion the sun.
       God said, "Let the earth put forth", and "the earth brought forth",   Gen 1:11,12
       and a day later – on the fourth day – He created the moon.
       After the seeds had sprouted along with the grasses on the third day,
       then the Lord made the moon on the fourth day.
1325   Vegetation sprouted forth and after that day the moon came into existence;
       in His wisdom [God] gave the moon a day to make [vegetation] sprout forth.
       Just as He gave the sun both light and heat,
       He granted the moon to make seeds sprout forth and flourish.
       These two ministers are constituted for the service of the Lord,

---

[25] See above, lines 1277–1280. See also Mathews, *Jacob of Sarug's Homilies on the Six Days of Creation: The Second Day*, 591–604, and idem., *Jacob of Sarug's Homilies on the Six Days of Creation: The Third Day*, 857–890, 925–936, 949–964, where even nature could not impede God's command, *et passim*.

[26] Deuteronomy 33:14, Pesh. Jacob seems to have lifted this directly from Ephrem, who cites the same verse in service of the same argument; see his *Commentary on Genesis* I.9.

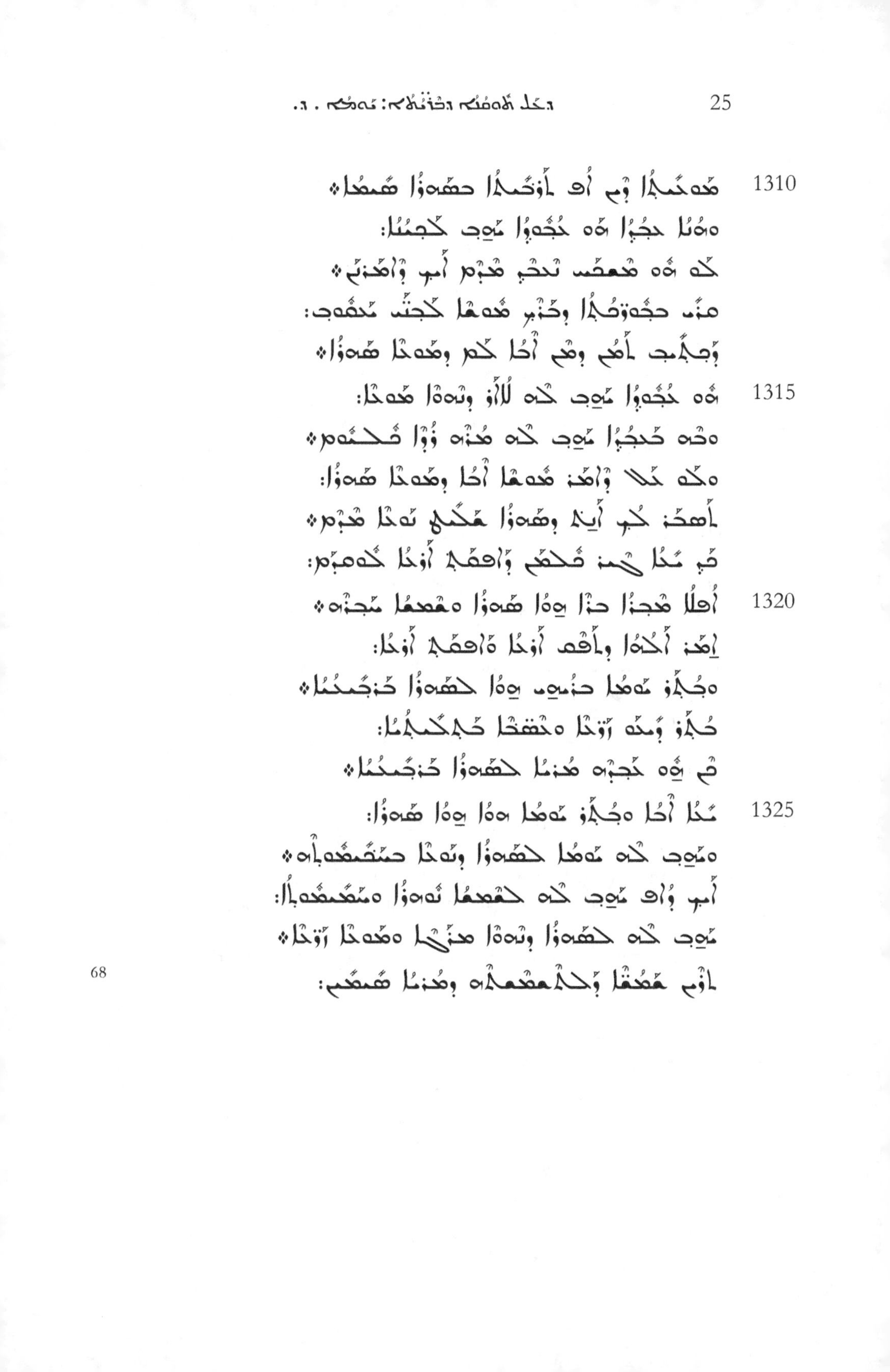

1330 so that one makes sprout while the other ripens, as they were
        commanded.
The moon moistens, causes to sprout and opens all vegetation,
then the sun comes and blows on it [giving it] brightness and a
        comely color.

V. THE MOON IS A TYPE OF A HUMAN BEING

[God] set the moon to wax, to wane and to change
that it might be a minister for the change of seasons.
1335 Although a blossom is small [the moon] causes it to grow,
and [the blossom] rises up by it until it becomes a large fruit.
It grows and rises up, it shrinks and falls down, it comes and it
        goes;
[God] depicts types by the course of its path while it changes.
It becomes an infant, then a young man, and [finally] an old man,
1340 and thus He paints an image for youth and old age.[27]
[The moon] is light when it waxes, dark as it wanes, [then] as if it
        were no more,
so that young people might look upon it and acquire humility.
Woe to you, O young one, who are light and puffed up like the
        moon,
Lo, old age [will be like] clouds of pain upon your head.
1345 Lo, the circle of your [life] has declined and diminished from its
        fullness,
you will decline, diminish, and will not exist among the handsome
        ones.
The skin of your face will become wrinkled and deteriorated,
your beauty will go away like the fullness of the moon that diminishes.
A young man resembles the full moon for he is completely full,

---

[27] Theophilus of Antioch, *Ad Autolycum*, II.15, albeit in the context of his anti-pagan polemic, also maintains that the sun and the moon are "a pattern and type (Gk., δεῖγμα καὶ τύπον) of God and mankind, respectively, though his description differs somewhat from that of Jacob. Basil, *Hexaemeron*, VI.2, rather asserts than argues the same point.

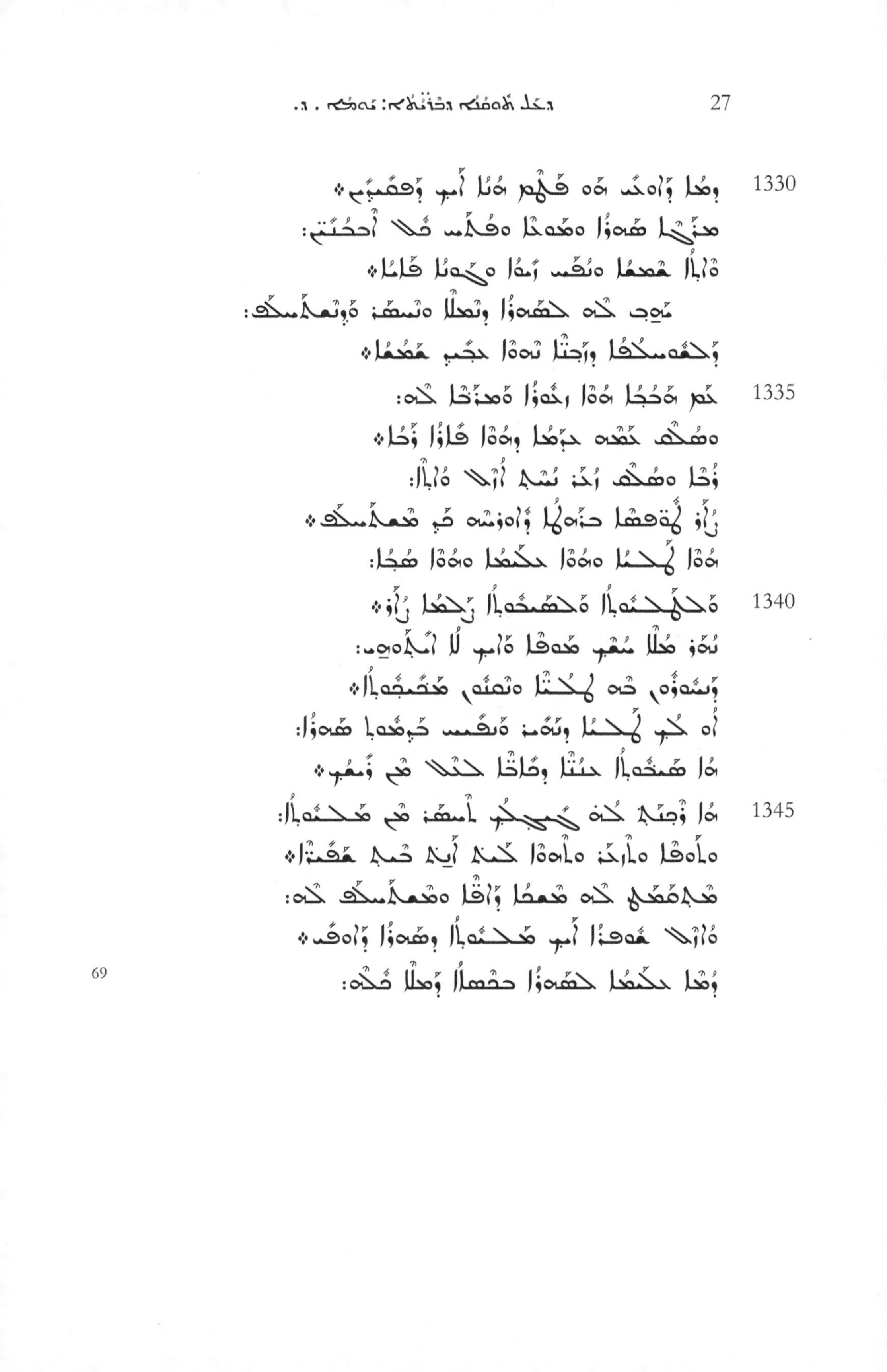

1350 but lo, when the eye begins to delight in his beauty he begins to diminish.
[The moon] begins to diminish, begins to descend, to become nothing,
in order to depict as a type youthfulness and its changes.
[Like] a full moon, O proud young person, your time is short,
you will become dark – humble yourself while you are light.
1355 The short time of life that comes to you will be completed,
but should anyone look upon that end he will not see you.
In the prime of life it is good to desist from your evils,
for then it is good for you to be enlightened by good things.
Consider that your fullest breath is at the first of the month – which is not long –,
1360 make your self repentant, and love silence more than evil.

VI. THE SUN IS A TYPE OF GOD

Look upon God, for He even depicts the sun as an image of Himself,
by its full light that does not change with the days.
All day it is large, all day it is strong, all day it is bright,
all day it is fully light and its rising is beautiful.[28]
1365 The sun is light, equally so at mid-month and at the first of the month,
for it neither diminishes nor increases more than its fullness.
Even of God it is said that "You are as You are",[29]
He exists just as [the sun] exists, and there are no others.
For this reason let the soul stand silently beside Him,

---

[28] The very same point is made in Theophilus of Antioch, *Ad Autolycum*, I.15.

[29] Psalm 102:28, Pesh.

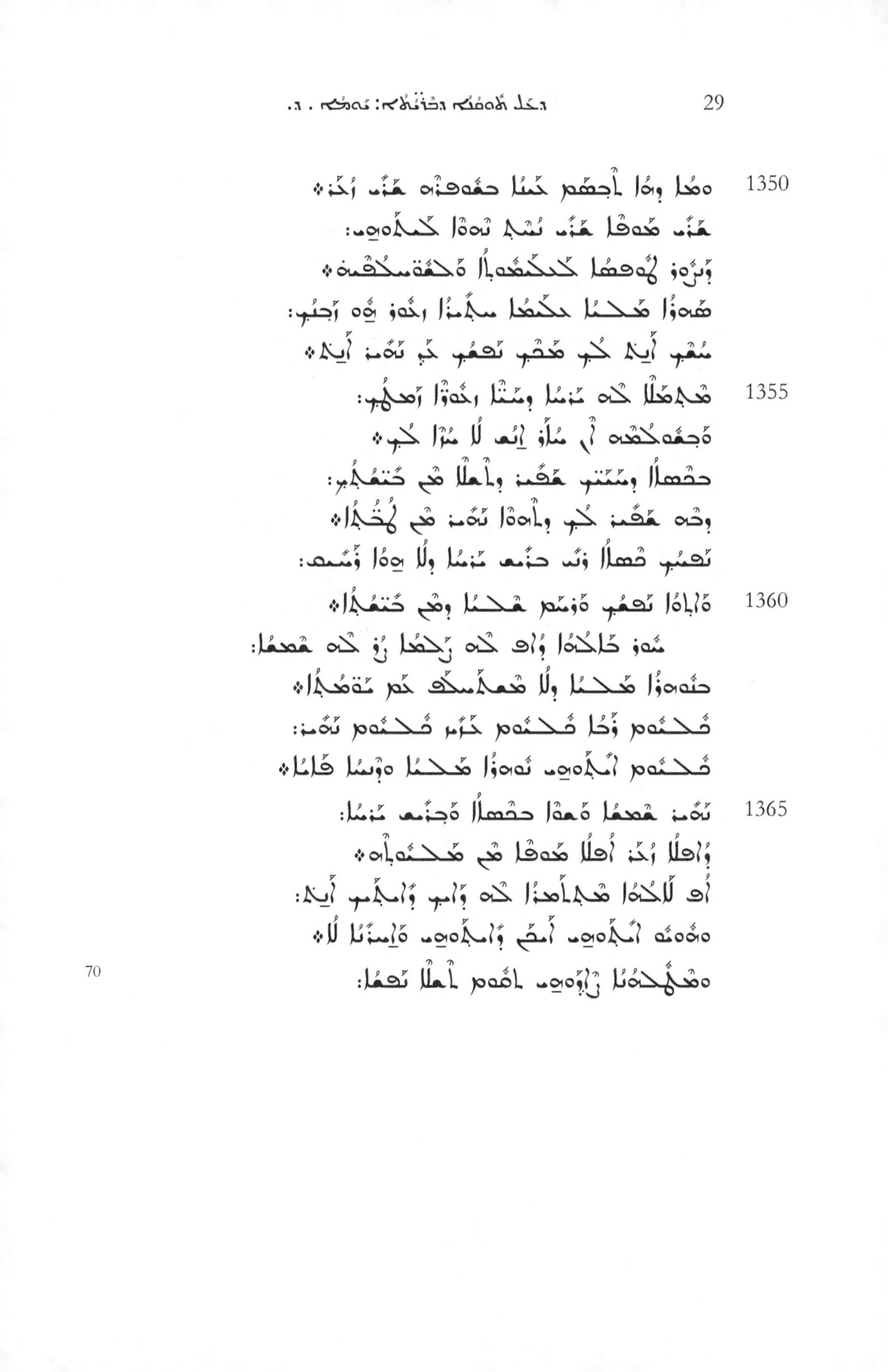

1370 gazing upon Him, taking pride in Him and being illuminated by Him.
It trusts in Him for He is the light that does not change,
and whoever relies on that trust in Him is illuminated by Him.
He created the luminaries and although they are light in their forms,
He is the light that gives the light to the luminaries.
1375 He continually gives light to the sun that it may take its delight in Him,
and if He neglected to give it [light], it would come to its end.
The Lord of creation lit a lantern and placed it in creation,
and that lantern continually seeks its oil from His goodness.
That One places light in it continually and makes it great,
1380 that its light might be sufficient to give light to the world that had been established.
[God] is that power that gives the sun the light to give light,
He casts the light into it continuously and makes it great.
In the same way, His power is bound to all the lights –
they receive their light from Him and then they give it to the earth.
1385 The intelligent one must constantly be looking upon [Him],
let him be amazed at the quick course of the hosts.
And let him give praise to that Maker who constituted them,
who yoked them and made them go swiftly along their paths.
With a numbering that was without confusion He arranged them,

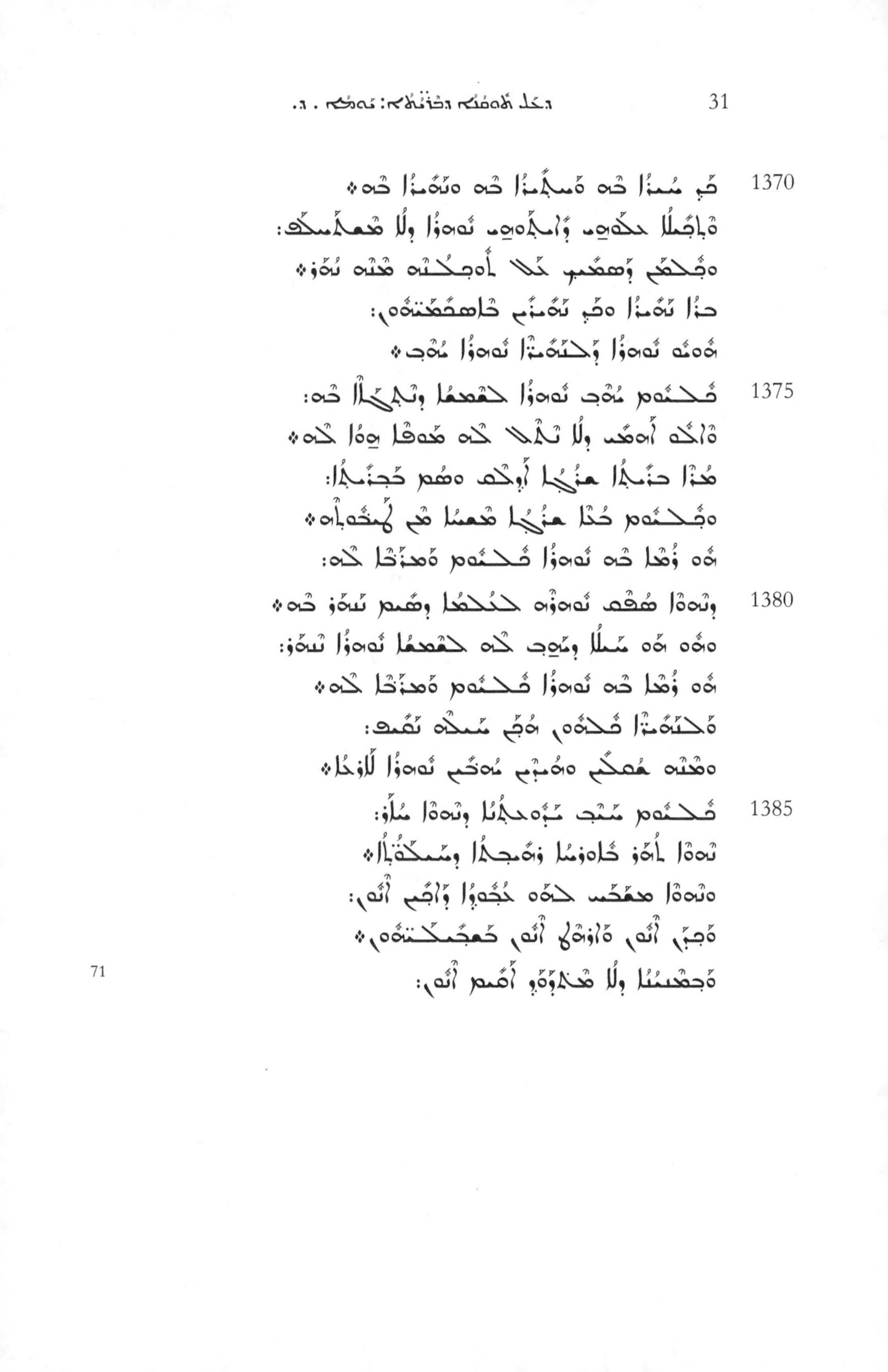

1390 He calls them and by their names they quickly take their place.
He harnessed Auriga[30] who carries the seasons and gave it speed,
and lo, it circulates alongside the courses [of others] and is not hindered.
His will is accomplished as He is the guide and He hastens it along,
that it may bear all the seasons through to the end.
1395 The Mighty One made Orion and the Pleiades[31] and guides them
on a southern path, and lo they are driven along it as they are commanded.
For this reason "the heavens proclaim the glory
of the Lord" at all times for the one who hears spiritually: Ps 19:1
for those wondrously beautiful things that constantly circulate along it,
1400 for those seasons that move along it one after the other,
for those courses of the hosts that are joined onto it,
with a quick eagerness that also comes from a mind with quick speed.

VII. THE HEAVENS PROCLAIM THE GLORY OF THE CREATOR

Because of these things, "Lo, the heavens proclaim the glory"   Ps 19:1
of that Maker who adorned them with every beauty.

---

[30] Known also as the "Charioteer" or the "Waggoner".

[31] [Ps.-] Ephrem cites both of these constellations in his *Commentary on Amos* 5:8; cited from M. Sokoloff, *A Syriac Lexicon*, 1095b.

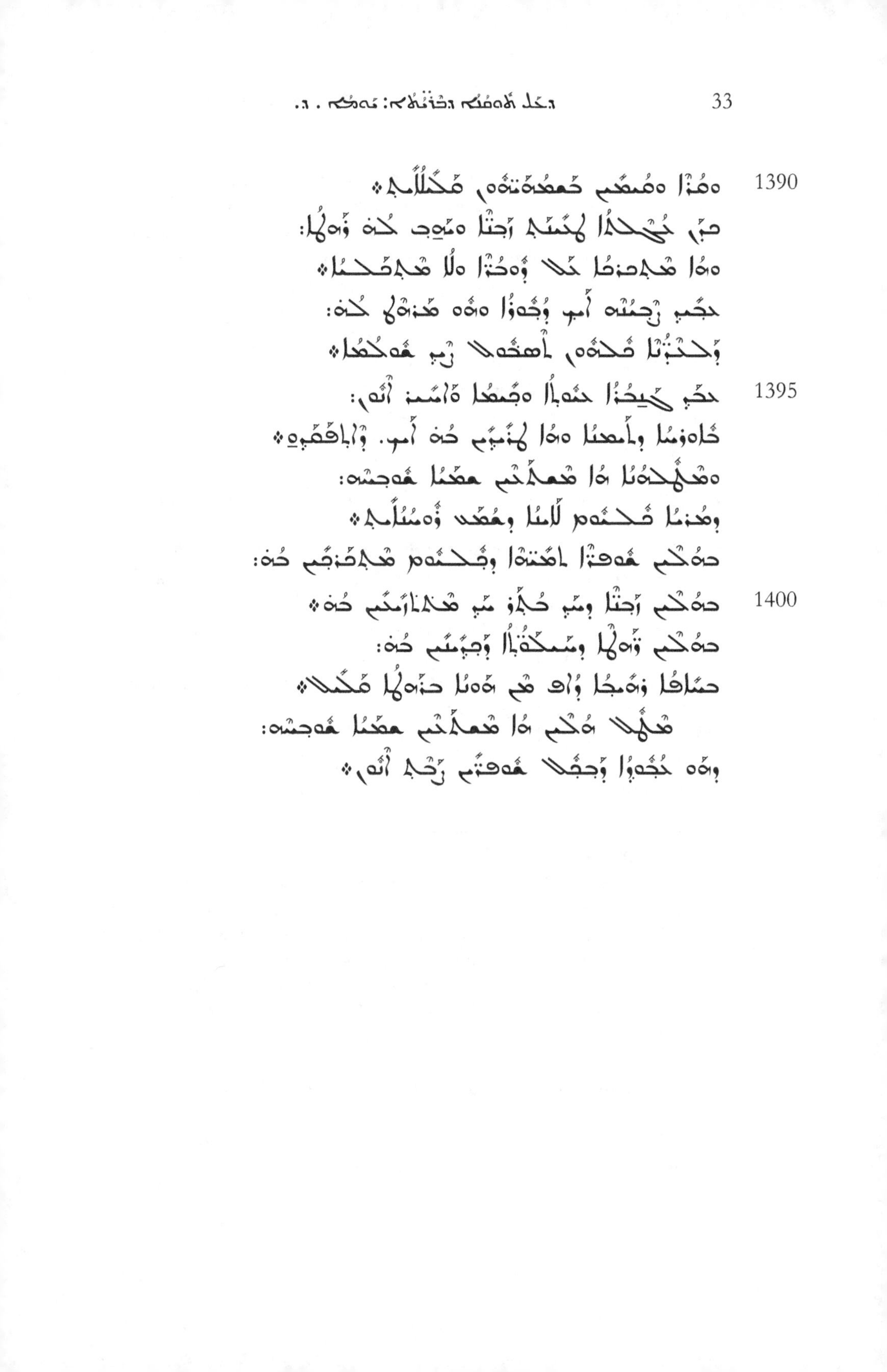

1405 Over the sun's light He exults and runs like a strong man,
and all the ends are included in the course of a day's journey,[32]
round about the world the head of whose path is outside the world,
and enclosed within it are the four corners and their boundaries.
It continually sets, it continually rises, it continually proceeds,
1410 it continually comes to rouse you to stand up and give [God] praise.
While you sleep you are idle and cool down,
but the sun, continually warm and in motion, stimulates you.
Come, heed and listen: "Behold, the heavens proclaim the glory
of the Lord", – your Lord! Thus, you too should respond and give [Him] glory.
1415 Lo, "the firmament makes known the work of His hands", but you do not notice   Ps 19:1
their beauties or their wonders as they are too many for you to see.
Lo, "the firmament makes known" to you "the work of the hands"
of His Creation[33],
by its vastness, and by the luminaries that have been set upon it.
Hear now that "behold, the heavens proclaim His glory";
1420 look and marvel at "the work of His hands" for it is full of wonder.
The firmament exists to show you – if you look upon it –
"the work" that is full of power and wisdom:
a great tent[34] that is full of the wonder of creation,[35]
and in it are the many wondrous courses of [God's] Making.[36]

---

[32] Cf. Psalm 19:5–6.

[33] Syr., *bôrûyûtô*; Jacob uses the abstract noun for God's creating and His making activity. I have noted each instance; cf. *Jacob of Sarug's Homily on The Third Day*, 5, and Jacob's own discussion of the different activities in *Jacob of Sarug's Homily on The Second Day*, 521–548.

[34] Cf. Psalm 19:5, Pesh., for this reference to tent; see also *Jacob of Sarug's Homily on The Second Day*, 552, 665, 791, and introduction, pp. 2–3, for similar terminology used by Jacob for the firmament in his *Homily on the Fashioning of Creation*.

[35] Syr., *bôrûyûtô*; cf. *Jacob of Sarug's Homily on The Third Day*, 5, and n. 33, above.

[36] Syr., *'ôbûdûtô*; cf. *Jacob of Sarug's Homily on The Third Day*, 5, and n. 33, above.

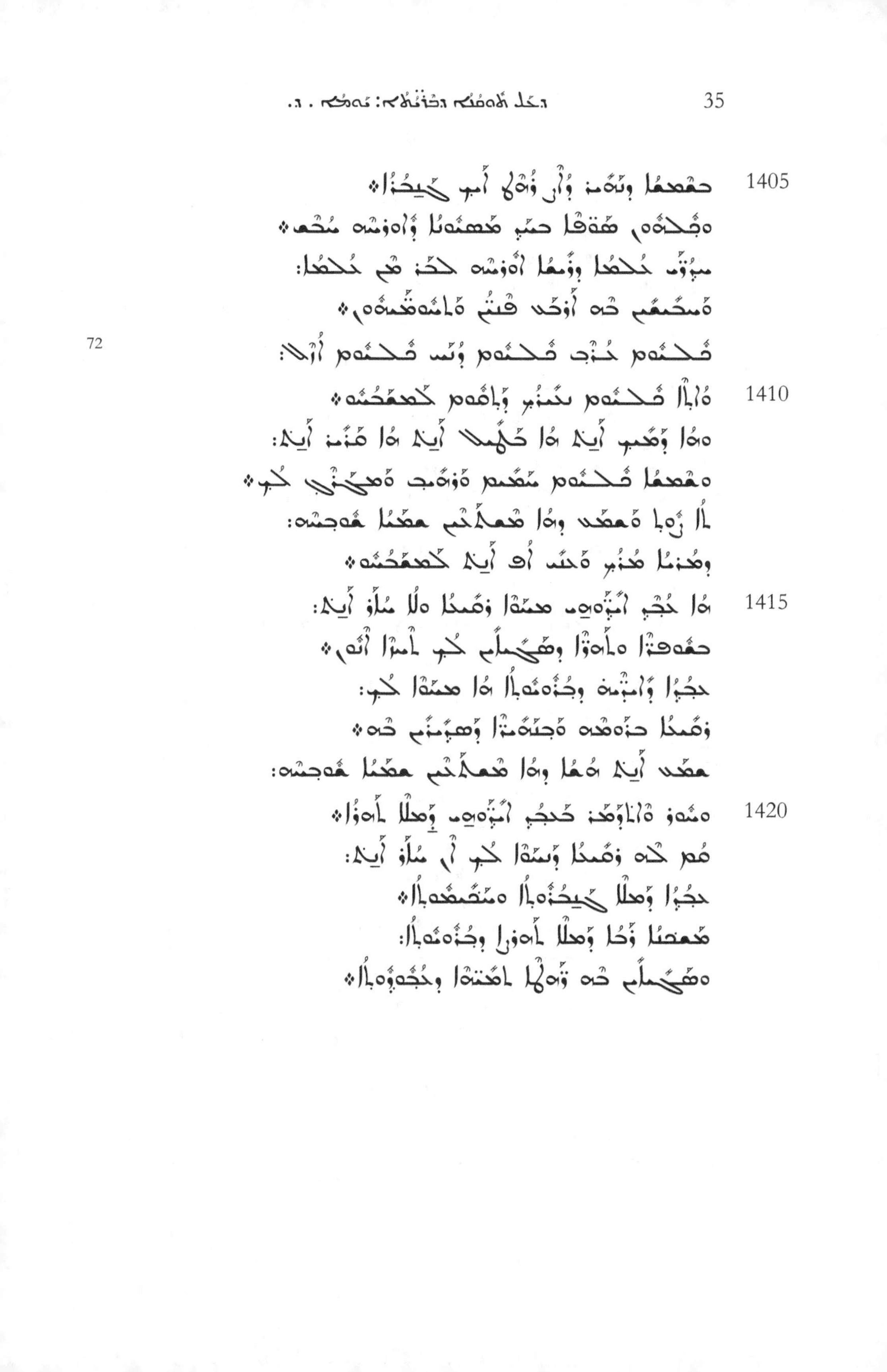

1425   The world has been yoked but it is a sphere full of movement,
it supports and raises up, it draws in and pushes out, but it is not restrained.
Lo, joined to it are nights and days,
dawns and evenings that open and close over all creation.
"The firmament makes known." Who does not look and see its beauties,
1430   apart from that one whose soul is blind and is full of darkness?
Lo, "the heavens proclaim His glory". And who does not hear,
except the hearing-impaired who is completely deaf to what is fitting.
The great course of hosts compels creatures,
and rouses them to "give glory" to that hidden power.[37]
1435   How glorious and how full of wonder is His mightiness!
And how wondrous in these beautiful things is His ability to make![38]

VIII.   ON THE FOURTH DAY GOD CREATED THE MOON FULL

On the fourth day [God] commanded and all the luminaries came to be,
and He guided them along a quick path one after the other.
He established them as rulers over the da[il]y cycles,
1440   and over the times of the nights and of the days.
And He had them lay hold of the gates of evening and the gates of dawn,[39]
so that they may open and close them over creation.
On the fourth day all the luminaries came into existence,
their watches began and they took control over their jurisdictions:

---

[37] Jacob, like Ephrem before him, considers it the duty of mankind to give God, their creator, praise at all times for His goodness; see also Mathews, *Jacob of Sarug's Homilies on the Six Days of Creation: The Third Day*, 1079–1080.

[38] Syr., *'ôbûdûtô*; cf. *Jacob of Sarug's Homily on The Third Day*, 5, and n. 33, above.

[39] *Jacob of Sarug's Homily on The Second Day*, 523, 827–830, had already introduced the image of evening and dawn as 'gates'.

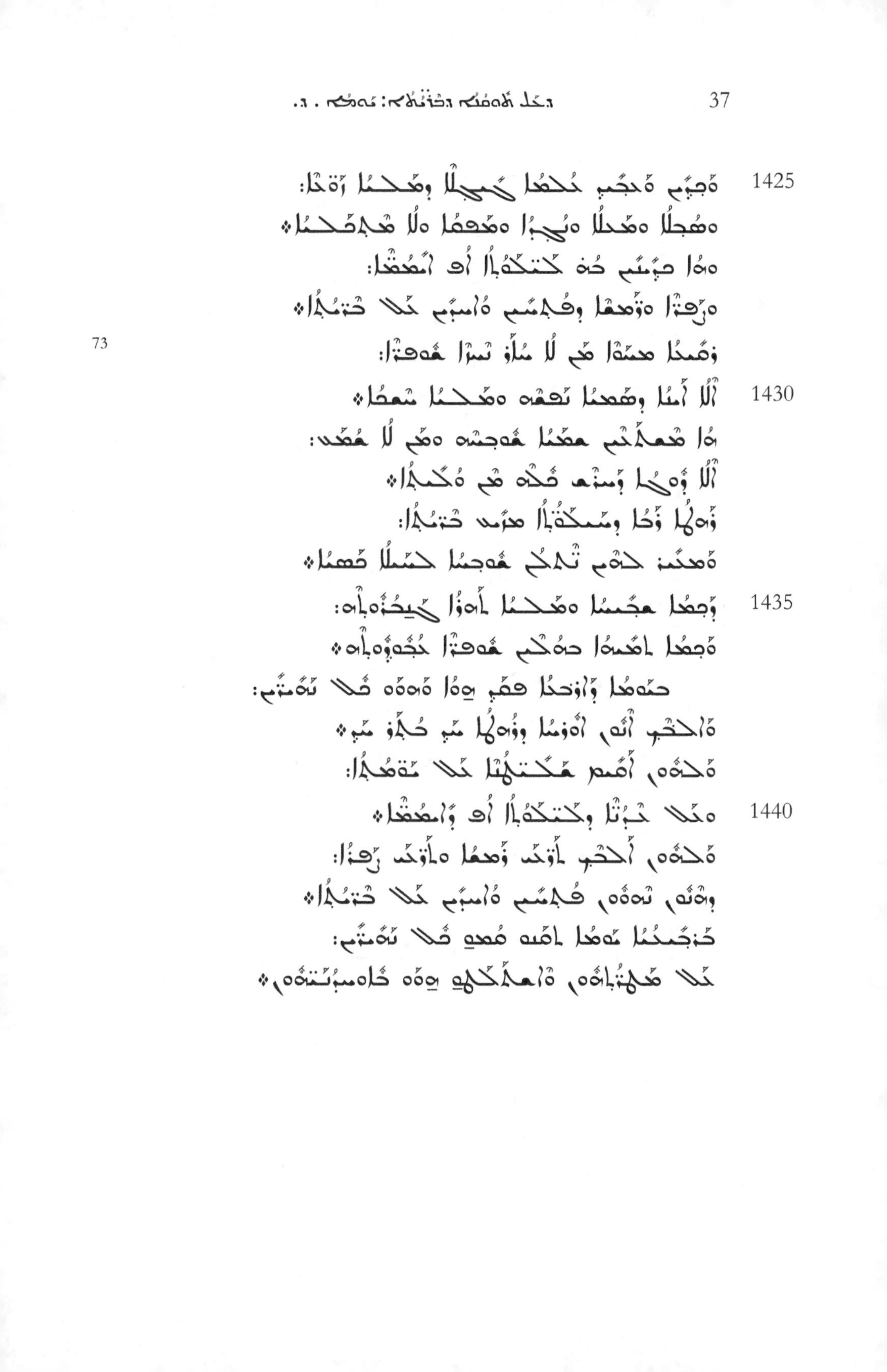

73

1445	the sun, the moon and all the stars by one command;	
	from one light His capacity to make[40] ordered this and set it down.	
	On the fourth day as at mid-month the moon came into existence,	
	its sphere was full just as the sun was full and complete.	
	He created the two great lights just as it is written,[41]	Gen 1:16
1450	therefore, it is clear that the moon was 'great', [that is] full and complete.[42]	

The moon was full, just as the fruits and trees[43] were,
and all their seeds were also complete and full just as they were.
The moon was full, so as soon as it came to be it began to wane,
that it might begin with the change of times, just as it had been commanded.

1455 It was made eleven days older than its yokemate,
for it came to be on the fourth day and was full and complete as at mid-month.[44]
Henceforth, therefore, those [four days] became these [fifteen],
it was wanting eleven days in a year and did not have them.
So, by this reckoning the sun had eleven additional days
1460 than the moon in the course of a year in which it was constituted.
That Maker did not will to make them equal and so yoke them,
because He sought to conduct them according to the changes [of time].
He set them for times, for signs as well as for years,
and for the change of all times that came along afterwards.

---

[40] Syr., *'ôbûdûtô*; cf. *Jacob of Sarug's Homily on The Third Day*, 5, and n. 33, above.

[41] Cf. also Psalm 136:7.

[42] See also, Eghishē, *Commentary on Genesis*, 26–27: *lusinn li steghtsaw*.

[43] Cf. Genesis 1:11. That everything was created "full-grown" was a teaching that Jacob seems once again to have inherited from Ephrem, see Mathews, *Jacob of Sarug's Homily on The Third Day*, 1041–1056, and n.38, though this teaching also seems to be widespread among Christian writers; see, e.g., Eghishē, *Commentary on Genesis*, 26–27.

[44] The creation of the moon on the fourth day plus the eleven days totals fifteen days, when the moon would have been at its fullest; see the fuller discussion of Ephrem in his *Commentary on Genesis*, I.23–24.

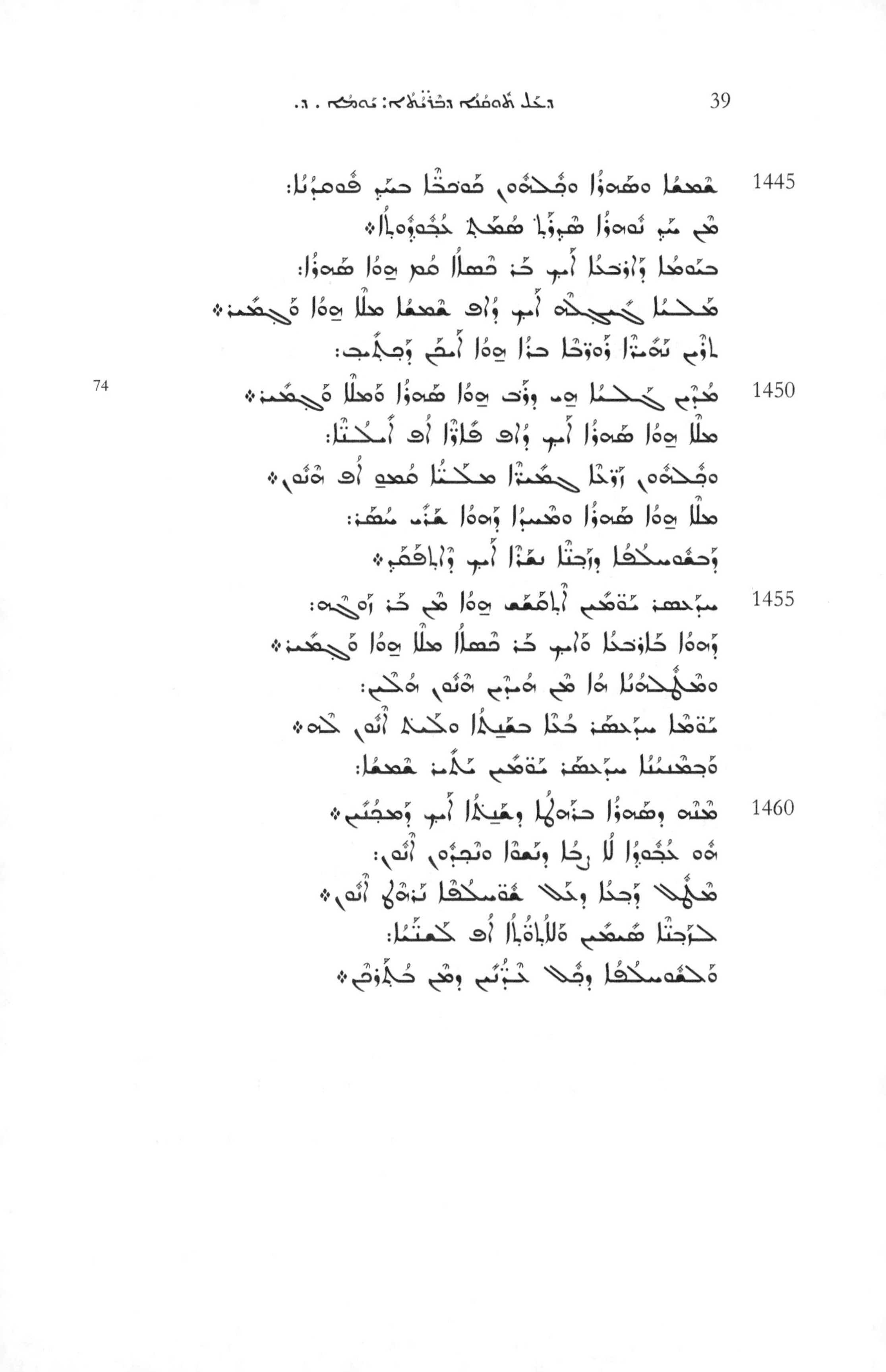

1465 For this reason He made them different, but He joined them wisely,
that by their course He might alter the times over creation.

IX. GOD SET THE LUMINARIES IN CONTINUOUS MOTION ALONG SPECIFIC COURSES

On the fourth day, [God] arranged the [luminaries] and established them,
and He joined them together for they began to move quickly.
On the fourth [day] that chariot harnessed to the light began its course,
1470 then on the twelfth [day] that moving sphere went forth to the world.
[His] might harnessed it and the signal[45] of the Godhead spurred it on,
it quickly went out according to the measures the King set down for it.
He granted it appointed times and passage ways and drove it to go out,
and lo, it has been moving for six thousand years and never been hindered,
1475 girding itself by the daylight and going out through it,
and accompanying it the entire day without being hindered.
Similarly during the night, from eventide it begins to move,
and under strong compulsion it goes along through it until the dawn.
It is not easy for it to be still during the night when it reaches it,

---

[45] As already noted in previous fascicles in this series, this signal is an essential element in the early Syrian understanding of how God created the earth, especially for Jacob; see K. Alwan, "Le 'remzo' selon la pensée de Jacques de Saroug," and T. Bou Mansour, *La théologie de Jacques de Saroug*, I, 11–33.

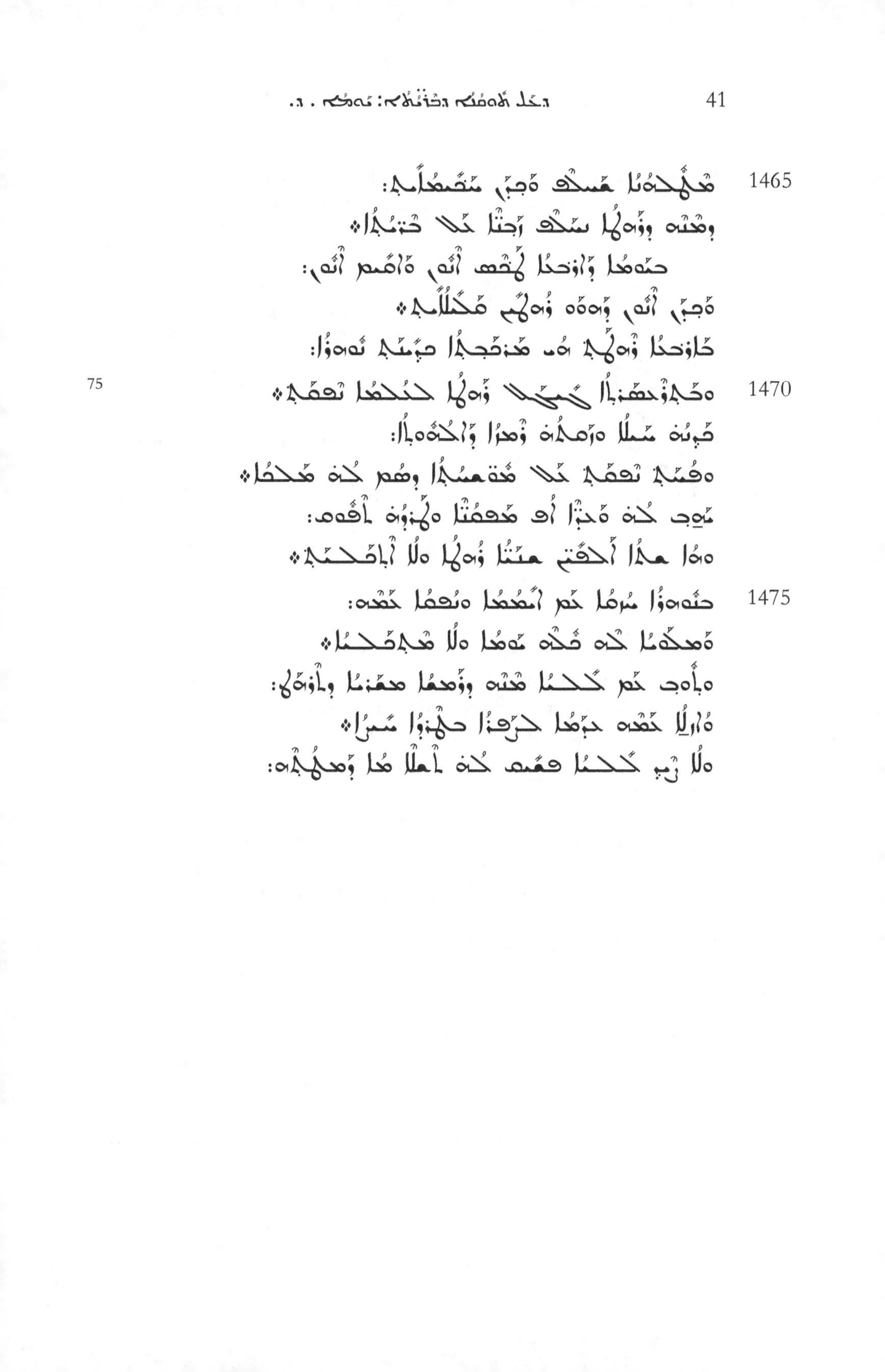

1480   nor does it know how to rest in the day when it encounters it.
       The cycle of night and day guides itself and has not been hindered
          from the time that [God's] hidden power that guides them joined them.
       Clear for all to see, the sun sits like a judge over [the day],
       while His hidden power is another governor along with it.
1485   From the moment He stirred it, after He harnessed it and gave it impetus,
       there was no need for Him to command it again to continue its course.
       At the beginning of the world, on the fourth day, He brought it in and harnessed it,
       and He set it up so that it continues to move so long as the world exists.
       Just as it was set up, it hearkened, it moved, sped up[46] and went out,
1490   and in this way it moves along that it might be still at the end of the world.
       Lo, the hosts that are yoked to [the firmament] are swift,
       and the sun and the moon that are bound to it hurry along with it.
       The stars, both small and great, that are joined to it also proceed,
       and with a single impetus they all move along though they are many.
1495   And along with the chariot of light that His Making[47] has yoked to it,
       the course of the hosts is entirely harnessed and bound.
       There are swift ones and there are slow ones, but one course,
       for the One who arranged them is wise and skillful and full of wonder.
       With these luminaries and the changes of seasons,

---

   [46] Syr., *pāḥat*, literally, "to blow, exhale". There is no variant here, so if this is the correct reading, I am not sure of its precise meaning, I opted for what sounded best in the context.

   [47] Syr., *'ôbûdûtô*; cf. *Jacob of Sarug's Homily on The Third Day*, 5, and n. 33, above.

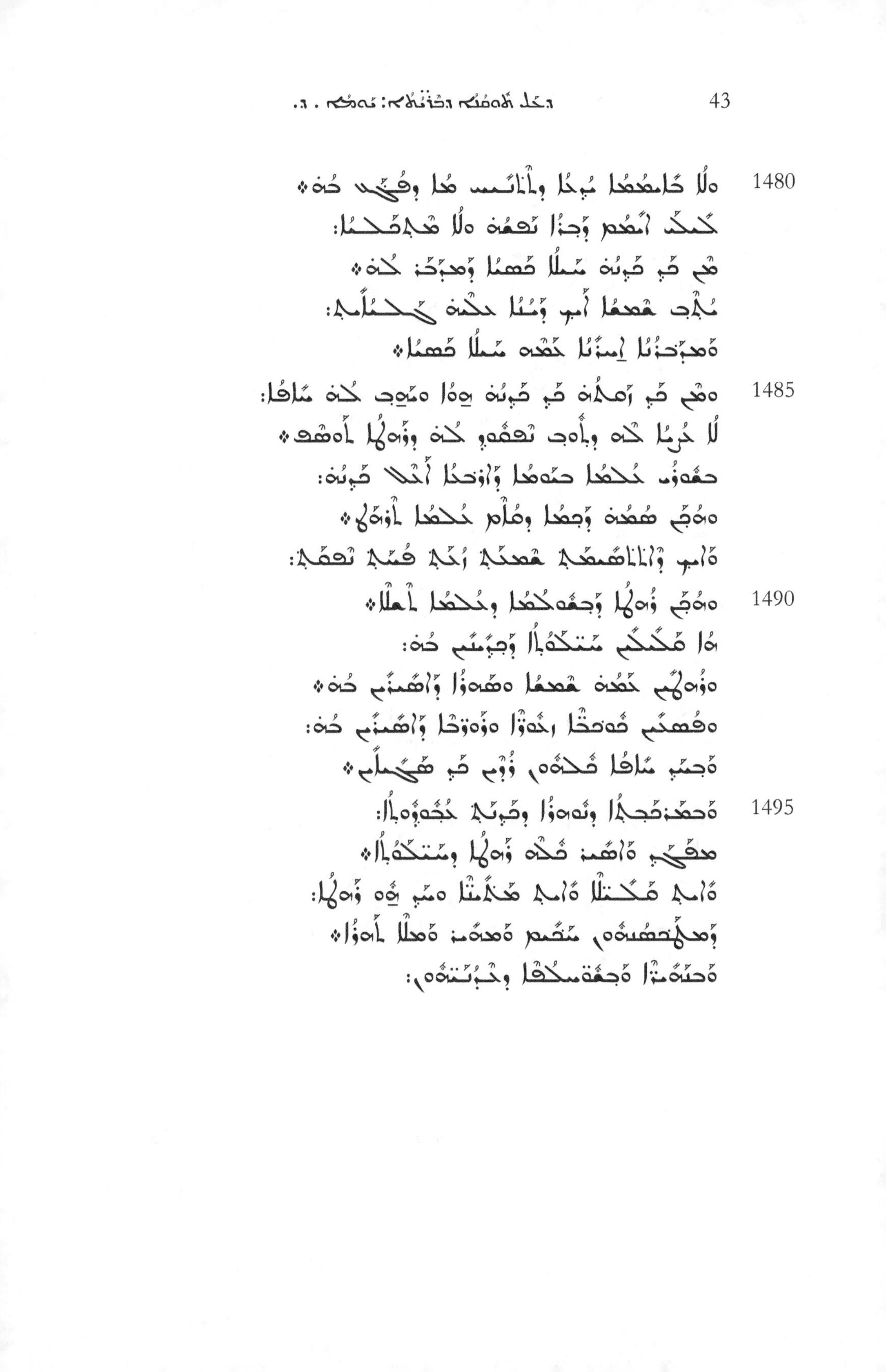

1500 He painted an image of how great is His capacity to make.[48]
"The firmament makes known the work of His hands" continually
    to the world,   Ps 19:1
and the one who recognizes it will truly see and marvel:
at these beauties and these marvels of all creation,
at these adornments and those things depicted on the firmament,
1505 at the course of the sun, its comeliness and its rays,
at the sphere of the moon and the changes that are moved by it,
at the light of the stars and the progression of their forms,
at the passage-way along which the powers make their way.

X. GOD GAVE TO EACH OF THE LUMINARIES ITS OWN PARTICULAR GLORY

From one light all these things were made though they are many,
1510 but they are not one in the multiplicity of their changes.
The glory of the sun is different from that of the luminaries,
for the great sea in which the light had been contained is boundless.
The glory of the moon is also different in how swift,
how fast and in what manner it proceeds along the ways.
1515 So too is the glory of the stars something different,
and even if one gazes on it alone, it causes him to marvel.
Each star possesses something more than its companion,
and if one were to seek it out it would fill his soul with wonder.
A small star, His handiwork, acts just as it was constituted,
1520 and thus all of them are placed as signs of the seasons.
Whether small or large the Wisdom on high has arranged them
like beautiful paintings on a huge vase.
Lo, they are full of beauties and glories, both exalted and lowly,
so that the Maker of the world might give them glory as He wills.

---

[48] Syr., *'ôbûdûtô*; cf. *Jacob of Sarug's Homily on The Third Day*, 5, and n. 33, above.

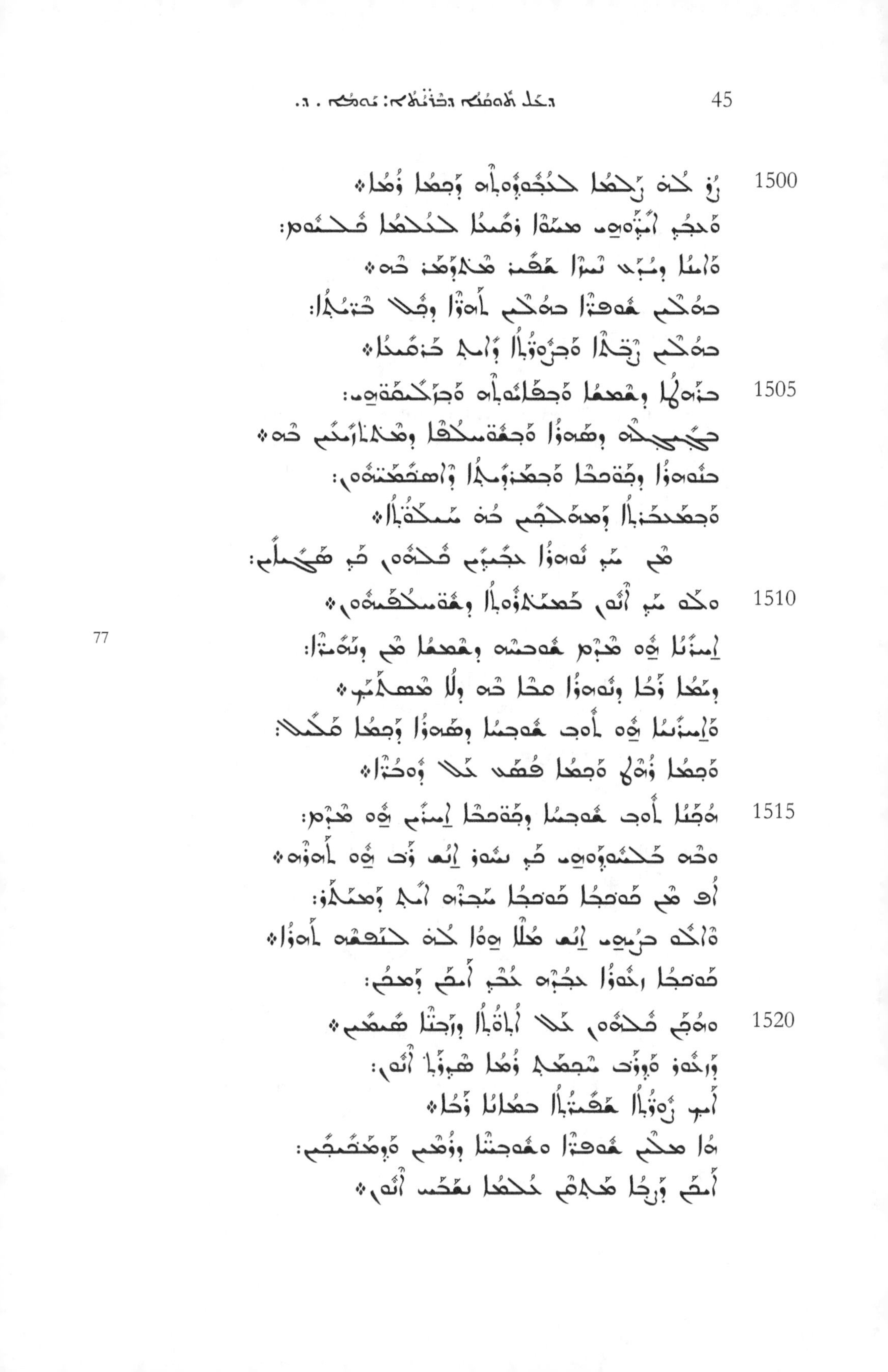

1525 To each one of them, just as He willed, He gave light,
and in proportion to the light its Lord gave it it was glorified.
That one to which He gave more light has more glory,
while to Him all the glories of all the luminaries are indebted.
To the large star there is great glory from those who see it,
1530 but apart from Him who wished it to be large, who is to be glorified?
To that Maker who made [them] large and small according to His will
belong all the glories and to Him they are to be given.
For from one light He determined to make all the luminaries,
all the spheres, and all the orbs that are on the firmament.
1535 The great ones and the small ones He divided up and arranged as He willed,
and on one course He yoked both the large and the little onto the firmament.
The glory of the sun and the glory of the moon both belong to Him,
and if a star is glorified for its light [that glory] is not its own.
Lo, they are bright, they are beautiful, they are many;
1540 and by their hosts, one [alone] is glorified: He who created them.

XI. God established the Times and Seasons by the Sun and the Moon

On the fourth day [God] established the [luminaries] at their posts,
and He made them move swiftly on the wide path He had prepared for them.
And He established the course of the daytime by the sun that shone forth,
and it was ordered according to twelve measures.
1545 And it acquired intervals of three and six and nine hours,
for it [previously] had no companions, nor spans nor measures.
The night was adorned with the moon and the stars that came to be,
and they pierce through the thick darkness with their rays.
The day shines forth for it possesses the King who directs it,

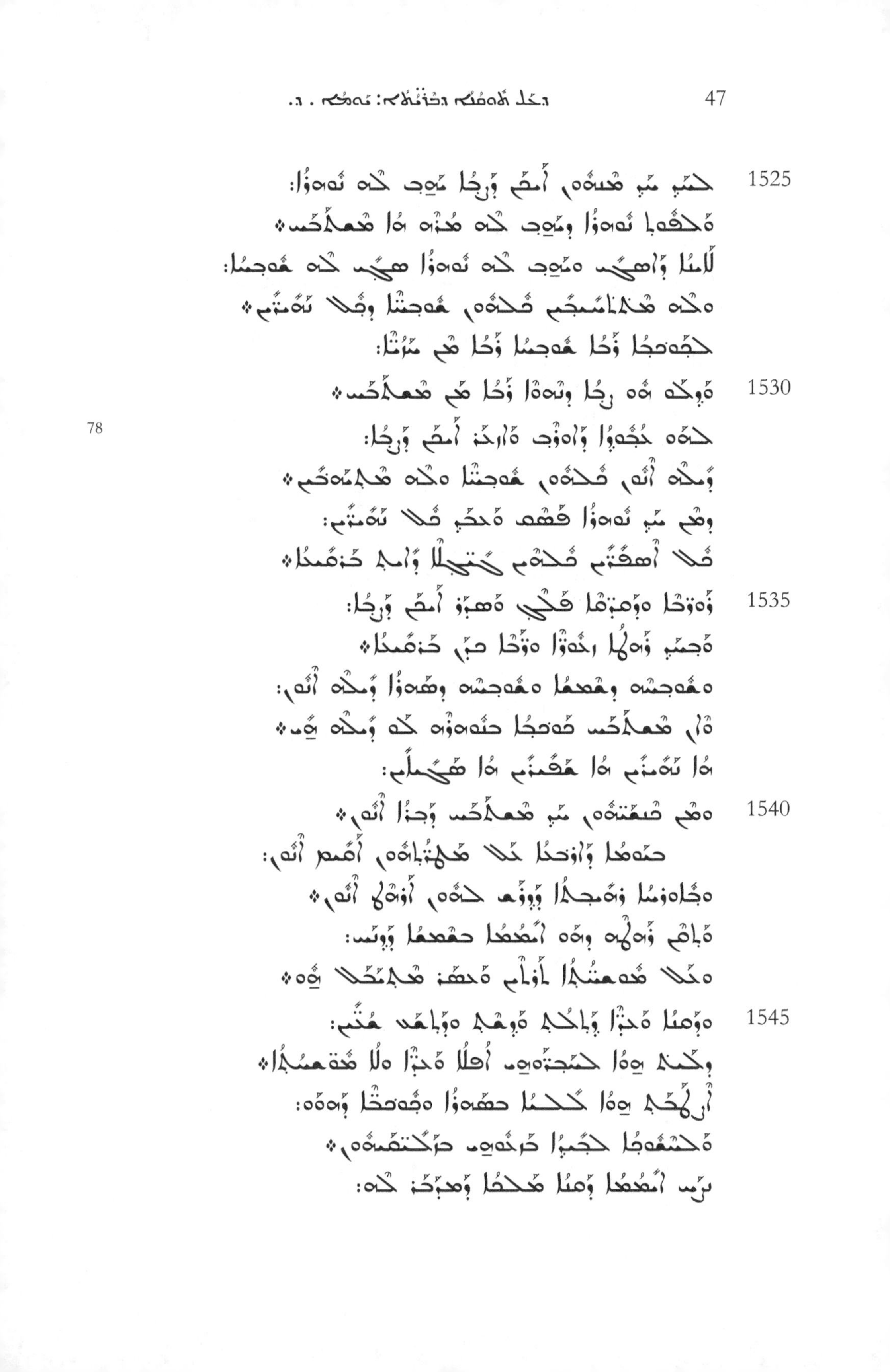

1550 and the night gives joy by the hosts that move about in it.
　　　Its Lord placed the sun as a crown with its dazzling rays,
　　　and He enriched the moon with the arrangement of the stars that accompany it.
　　　It is at peace in the presence of the night along with those hosts
　　　that latched onto that path to proceed along the passage way.
1555 The day exulted when the sun went out to walk in it,
　　　and with the measurements and intervals that He set for it He granted it peace.
　　　The east jumped for joy for it knelt down and gave birth to a mighty warrior:
　　　the sun that rose from it and gave light to the entire earth.
　　　The south rejoiced for it had become a path for the hosts,
1560 and just as on the waves of the sea it sailed by its lights.
　　　The west rejoiced for they were gathered into it as if into a harbor,
　　　and they set in it in order to give way and become night.
　　　The north gave glory to that One who constructed such high mountains in it,
　　　and made it a hiding place for the sun to pass into, to go away and to rise again.
1565 All four corners of the world give glory with wonder,
　　　"and there was evening and there was morning, the fourth [day]." Gen 1:19

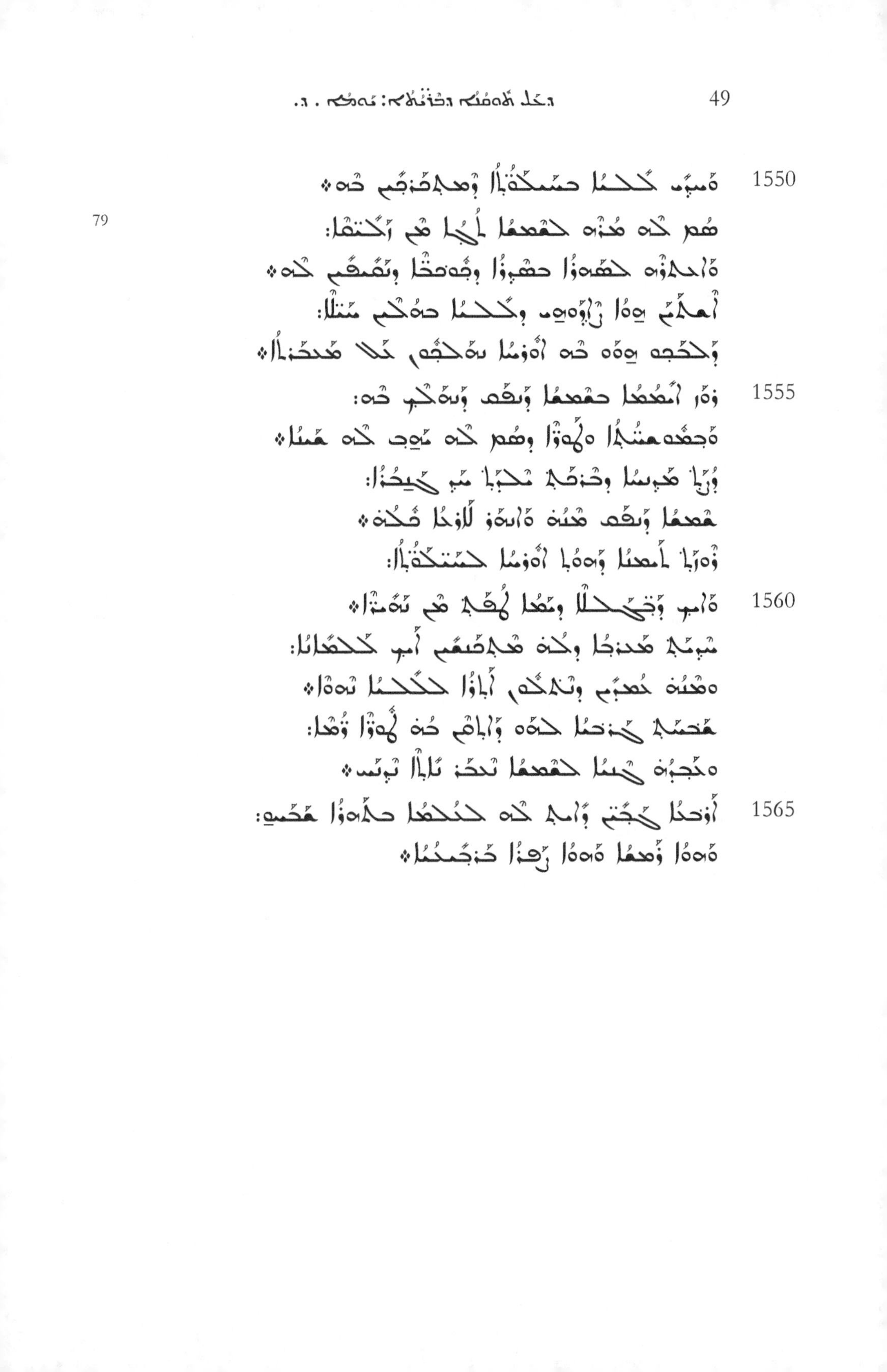

BIBLIOGRAPHY OF WORKS CITED

PRIMARY TEXTS

THEOPHILUS OF ANTIOCH

Grant, Robert M., ed. and tr. *Theophilus of Antioch, Ad Autolycum.* Oxford Early Christian Texts; Oxford: Clarendon Press, 1970.

EUSEBIUS OF EMESA

Petit, Françoise, Lucas Van Rompay and Jos. J.S. Weitenberg, trs. *Eusèbe d'Émèse, Commentaire de la Genèse.* Traditio Exegetica Graeca, 15; Louvain: Peeters, 2011.

BASIL

Giet, Stanislas, ed. *Saint Basile, Homélies sur l'Hexaméron.* Sources Chrétiennes, 26bis; Paris: Editions du Cerf, 1968. English translation in Blomfield Jackson, tr., *The Hexaemeron of Saint Basil.* A Select Library of Nicene and Post-Nicene Fathers. Second Series. Grand Rapids, 1976. Vol. 8, pp. 52–107.

Thomson, Robert W., ed. and tr. *The Syriac Version of the Hexaemeron by Basil of Caesarea.* CSCO 550–551; Louvain: Peeters, 1995.

EPHREM

Tonneau, Raymond M., ed. *Sancti Ephraem Syri in Genesim et in Exodum commentarii.* CSCO 152–53. Louvain: Peeters, 1955. English translation by Edward G. Mathews, Jr. in Edward G. Mathews, Jr. and Joseph P. Amar, *St. Ephrem the Syrian: Selected Prose Works.* Fathers of the Church, 91; Washington: Catholic University of America Press, 1994. Pp. 67–213.

THEODORET OF CYRUS

Hill, Robert C., ed. and tr. *Theodoret of Cyrus, The Questions on the Octateuch. Volume 1: On Genesis and Exodus*. Library of Early Christianity, 1; Washington: Catholic University Press, 2007.

EGHISHĒ

Khachikyan, Levon, ed. and Michael Papazian, tr. *Commentary on Genesis by Eghishe*. Yerevan: Magaghat Publishing House, 2004.

JACOB OF SARUG

Bedjan, Paulus, ed. (with additional material by Sebastian P. Brock). *Homilies of Mar Jacob of Sarug*. 6 vols.; Piscataway: Gorgias Press, 2006 [original publication *Homiliae Selectae Mar-Jacobi Sarugensis*, 5 vols. Paris and Leipzig: Harrassowitz, 1905–1910].

Mathews, Jr., Edward G. *Jacob of Sarug's Homilies on the Six Days of Creation: The First Day*. Texts from Christian Late Antiquity, 27; Metrical Homilies of Mar Jacob of Sarug, 29. Piscataway: Gorgias Press, 2009.

Mathews, Jr., Edward G. *Jacob of Sarug's Homilies on the Six Days of Creation: The Second Day*. Texts from Christian Late Antiquity, 40. Piscataway: Gorgias Press, 2016.

Mathews, Jr., Edward G. *Jacob of Sarug's Homilies on the Six Days of Creation: The Third Day*. Texts from Christian Late Antiquity, 47. Piscataway: Gorgias Press, 2016.

NARSAI

Gignoux, Philippe, ed. and tr. *Homélies de Narsaï sur la création*. Patrologia Orientalis, 34.3–4 [161–162]. Turnhout: Brepols, 1968.

OTHER

Petit, Françoise, ed. *Catenae Graece in Genesim et in Exodum II. Collectio Coisliniana in Genesim*. Corpus Christianorum Series Graeca, 15. Brepols: Turnhout, 1986.

SECONDARY WORKS

Alexandre, Monique. *Le commencement du livre Genèse I–V: La version grecque de la Septante et sa réception*. Christianisme Antique, 3. Paris: Beauchesne, 1988.

Alwan, Khalil. "Le 'remzo' selon la pensée de Jacques de Saroug." *Parole de l'Orient* 15 (1988–1989), 91–106.

Barsoum, Ignatius Aphram I. *The Scattered Pearls: A History of Syriac Literature and Sciences*. Second Revised Edition. Piscataway: Gorgias Press, 2003.

Bou Mansour, Tanios. *La théologie de Jacques de Saroug. Tome I: Création, Anthropologie, Ecclésiologie et Sacraments*. Bibliothèque de l'Université Saint-Esprit, 36; Kaslik: l'Université Saint-Esprit, 1993.

Brock, Sebastian, "Clothing metaphors as a means of theological expression in Syriac tradition." In Margot Schmidt, ed., *Typus, Symbol, Allegorie bei den östlichen Vätern und ihren Parallelen im Mittelalter*. Eichstatter Beiträge IV. Regensburg: Verlag Friedrich Pustet, 1982. Pp. 11–40; reprinted in Sebastian Brock, *Studies in Syriac Christianity*. Collected Studies Series, CS357. London: Variorum, 1992.

Ginzberg, Louis. *The Legends of the Jews*. Volumes I, V. New York: Jewish Publication Society, 1909, 1913.

Jansma, Taeke. "L'Hexaméron de Jacques de Sarug." *L'Orient Syrien* 4 (1959), 3–42, 129–162, 253–284.

Jansma, Taeke. "Une homélie anonyme sur la création du monde." *L'Orient Syrien* 5 (1960), 385–400.

Kronholm, Tryggve. *Motifs from Genesis 1–11 in the Genuine Hymns of Ephrem the Syrian with particular reference to the influence of Jewish exegetical tradition*. Coniectanea Biblica. Old Testament Series, 11. Uppsala: Almqvist & Wiksell, 1978.

Sokoloff, Michael. *A Syriac Lexicon. A Translation from the Latin, Correction, Expansion, and Update of C. Brockelmann's Lexicon Syriacum*. Piscataway: Gorgias Press/Winona Lake: Eisenbrauns, 2009.

Taylor, Richard A. *The Peshitta of Daniel*. Monographs of the Peshitta Institute Leiden, 7. Leiden: E.J. Brill, 1994.

ten Napel, Erik. "Some Remarks on the Hexaemeral Literature in Syriac." In Hans J.W. Drijvers, Rene Lavenant, Collie Molenberg and Gerrart J. Reinink, eds. *IV Symposium Syriacum: Literary Genres in Syriac Literature*. Orientalia Christiana Analecta, 229. Rome: Pontificium Institutum Studiorum Orientalium, 1987. Pp. 57–69.

INDEX

NAMES AND THEMES

references are to line numbers

Auriga   1391

beauty   1348, 1350, 1404
boundary   1220, 1225
brightness   1213, 1332

capacity to make (see also 'making')   1446, 1500
Chaldeans   1249, 1262, 1265, 1273, 1285, 1291
change   1206, 1210, 1216, 1245, 1333, 1334, 1338, 1352, 1362, 1371, 1454, 1462, 1464, 1499, 1506, 1510
chariot   1469, 1495
cold   1217, 1303
command   1193, 1212, 1244, 1286, 1295, 1298, 1330, 1396, 1437, 1445, 1454, 1486
course   1186, 1196, 1216, 1219, 1231, 1245, 1249, 1338, 1386, 1392, 1401, 1406, 1424, 1433, 1460, 1466, 1469, 1486, 1496, 1497, 1505, 1536, 1543
creation   1193, 1297, 1299, 1377, 1417, 1423, 1428, 1442, 1466, 1503

Creator   1261, 1264, 1281, 1299, 1311
creature   1210, 1433
cycle   1218, 1439, 1481

darkness   1207, 1230, 1430, 1548
dawn   1227, 1237, 1428, 1441, 1478
day   1188, 1189, 1198, 1199, 1201, 1205, 1213, 1218, 1326, 1362, 1363, 1364, 1406, 1427, 1441, 1455, 1457, 1458, 1459, 1470, 1476, 1480, 1481, 1483, 1549, 1555
  fourth day   1181, 1214, 1235, 1236, 1239, 1322, 1324, 1325, 1437, 1443, 1447, 1456, 1467, 1469, 1487, 1541, 1566
  third day   1323
dome   1196

east   1231, 1234, 1237, 1557
evening   1428, 1441, 1566

gate   1441
globe   1219, 1256
glory   1272, 1276, 1282, 1397, 1403, 1413, 1414, 1419,

1431, 1434, 1511, 1513,
1515, 1524, 1527, 1529,
1537, 1538, 1565
God   1183, 1186, 1189, 1212,
1303, 1321, 1326, 1333,
1338, 1361, 1367, 1381,
1410, 1424, 1437, 1467,
1482, 1541
Godhead   1257, 1471
governance   1247, 1259
governor   1268, 1484
grass   1323

heat   1217, 1281, 1308, 1327
heaven   1242, 1397, 1403,
1413, 1419, 1431
host   1242, 1253, 1386, 1401,
1433, 1491, 1496, 1540,
1550, 1553, 1559

interval   1188, 1545, 1556

Jacob   1313
judge   1199, 1483

king   1185, 1269, 1472, 1549

light   1182, 1193, 1195, 1201,
1209, 1211, 1212, 1213,
1224, 1225, 1228, 1327,
1341, 1343, 1354, 1362,
1364, 1365, 1371, 1373,
1374, 1375, 1376, 1379,
1380, 1381, 1382, 1383,
1384, 1405, 1446, 1459,
1469, 1495, 1507, 1509,
1512, 1525, 1526, 1527,
1533, 1538, 1558, 1560
Lord   1181, 1269, 1279, 1284,
1286, 1294, 1297, 1316,
1324, 1329, 1377, 1398,
1414, 1526, 1551
luminary   1181, 1183, 1185,
1197, 1202, 1214, 1239,
1241, 1373, 1374, 1418,
1437, 1443, 1467, 1499,
1511, 1528, 1533, 1541

Maker   1215, 1277, 1315, 1387,
1404, 1461, 1524, 1531
making (see also 'capacity to
make'   1424, 1495
measure   1472, 1544, 1546,
1556
minister   1200, 1206, 1301,
1329, 1334
moon   1184, 1186, 1191, 1200,
1211, 1301, 1302, 1303,
1310, 1314, 1317, 1318,
1320, 1322, 1324, 1325,
1326, 1328, 1331, 1333,
1335, 1341, 1343, 1348,
1349, 1351, 1353, 1445,
1447, 1450, 1451, 1453,
1460, 1492, 1506, 1513,
1537, 1547, 1552
month   1359, 1365, 1447, 1457
morning   1566
Moses   1313, 1317

name   1235, 1240, 1243, 1390
nature   1267, 1277, 1279, 1297,
1311, 1312
night   1191, 1198, 1200, 1205,
1218, 1427, 1440, 1477,
1479, 1481, 1547, 1550,
1553, 1562
north   1233, 1234, 1563

orb   1196, 1249, 1534
Orion   1395

path   1192, 1204, 1218, 1222,
1231, 1233, 1239, 1242,
1258, 1338, 1388, 1396,
1407, 1438, 1542, 1554,
1559
Pleiades   1395

INDEX

power   1257, 1260, 1283, 1293, 1381, 1383, 1422, 1434, 1482, 1484, 1508

region   1207, 1224, 1232, 1235, 1236, 1240
ruler   1189, 1191, 1198, 1205, 1270, 1294, 1297, 1439

season   1187, 1206, 1217, 1245, 1334, 1391, 1394, 1400, 1499, 1520
seed   1323, 1328, 1452
service   1202, 1300, 1329
sign   1187, 1463, 1520
signal   1471
south   1231, 1234, 1396, 1559
sphere   1182, 1194, 1215, 1425, 1448, 1470, 1506, 1534
star   1184, 1187, 1192, 1197, 1200, 1211, 1243, 1261, 1269, 1271, 1445, 1493, 1507, 1515, 1517, 1519, 1529, 1538, 1547, 1552
summer   1217, 1246
sun   1184, 1185, 1189, 1199, 1211, 1221, 1237, 1238, 1301, 1302, 1305, 1308, 1309, 1321, 1327, 1332, 1361, 1365, 1368, 1375, 1381, 1405, 1412, 1445, 1448, 1459, 1483, 1492, 1505, 1511, 1537, 1543, 1551, 1555, 1558, 1564

time   1188, 1227, 1261, 1353, 1355, 1398, 1440, 1454, 1462, 1463, 1464, 1466, 1473, 1482
type   1338, 1352

vegetation   1302, 1304, 1306, 1307, 1309, 1314, 1317, 1325, 1326, 1331

wane   1333, 1341, 1453
west   1232, 1234, 1238, 1561
will   1284, 1393, 1524, 1525, 1531, 1535
winter   1217, 1246
wisdom   1248, 1255, 1274, 1326, 1422, 1521
wonder   1219, 1416, 1420, 1423, 1435, 1498, 1518, 1565
work   1415, 1417, 1420, 1422, 1501,
world   1202, 1204, 1216, 1223, 1226, 1266, 1300, 1380, 1407, 1425, 1470, 1487, 1488, 1490, 1501, 1524, 1565

year   1188, 1458, 1460, 1463, 1474

Zodiac   1260

BIBLICAL REFERENCES

References are to page number

Genesis
   1:3 — 12
   1:11 — 24, 38
   1:12 — 24
   1:14 — 8
   1:16 — 8, 9, 10, 38
   1:14–19 — 2
   1:19 — 48

Deuteronomy
   4:19 — 18
   33:14 — 24

1 Kings
   18:38 — 20

Psalms
   19:1 — 4, 32, 34, 44
   19:5 — 14, 34
   19:6 — 14, 34
   102:28 (Pesh) — 28
   136:7 — 38
   136:8 — 9
   136:9 — 10
   147:4 — 14

Wisdom of Solomon
   13:1–9 — 18

Daniel
   3:21 — 20
   3:49 (LXX/Pesh) — 20

Hebrews
   13:8 — 4

www.ingramcontent.com/pod-product-compliance
Lightning Source LLC
Chambersburg PA
CBHW070304230426
43664CB00014B/2630